Spiritual Intimacy
for Couples

CHARLES AND VIRGINIA SELL

CROSSWAY BOOKS • WHEATON, ILLINOIS
A DIVISION OF GOOD NEWS PUBLISHERS

Spiritual Intimacy for Couples

Copyright © 1996 by Charles and Virgina Sell

Published by Crossway Books
  A division of Good News Publishers
  1300 Crescent Street
  Wheaton, Illinois 60187

Cover photo: Jim Whitmer

Cover design: Cindy Kiple

First printing, 1996

Printed in the United States of America

Scripture taken from the HOLY BIBLE: NEW INTERNATIONAL VERSION®. Copyright © 1973, 1978, 1984 by International Bible Society. Used by permission of Zondervan Publishing House. All rights reserved.

The "NIV" and "New International Version" trademarks are registered in the United States Patent and Trademark Office by International Bible Society. Use of either trademark requires the permission of International Bible Society.

Library of Congress Cataloging-in-Publication Data
Sell, Charles M., 1933-
    Spiritual intimacy for couples / Charles and Virginia Sell.
        p.   cm.
    ISBN 0-89107-888-6
    1. Married people—Religious life.   2. Spiritual life—
Christianity.   3. Intimacy (Psychology)—Religious aspects—
Christianity.   I. Sell, Virginia.   II. Title.
BV4596.M3S35   1996
248.8'44—dc20   96-548

05	04	03	02	01	00	99	98	97	96
15	14	13	12	11	10	9	8	7	6	5	4	3	2	1

For
all our friends

Contents

Acknowledgments   ix

Preface xi

1 Spiritually Two-gether   15

2 Worshiping Two-gether   33

3 Celebrating Two-gether   67

4 Praying Two-gether   95

5 Studying Two-gether   123

6 Growing Two-gether   151

Additional Resources   183

Notes   187

Acknowledgments

We thank the many husbands and wives who contributed to our survey of the spiritual lives of Christian couples. Their evaluation of their own experience along with practical suggestions greatly enrich this book.

We are grateful to Len Goss and the staff of Crossway Books for recognizing the new awareness among couples to improve the spiritual side of their relationship and share our vision to help them to do so. Special thanks to Steve Hawkins who did the behind-the-scenes editing of the manuscript.

Preface

D eeper love." That's the phrase Becky used to explain how relating spiritually made her and her husband feel toward each other. They are among countless couples who are discovering how relating to God together impacts their marriage. Spiritual renewal for twos is in. "We're on a spiritual high," gushed one woman.[1] As never before, couples are attending retreats, watching videos, and reading books about spiritual oneness. They want to learn to pray and study the Bible together to grow spiritually, and in the process improve their marriage commitment and relationship.

We believe their hope is not in vain. We, Ginger and Chick (short for Virginia and Charles), have always believed that God is the best ally a married couple has. Over twenty years, in hundreds of marriage seminars, we've included a session on spiritual *togetherness*, convinced it is one of the most important components of a good marriage. A recent broadly based national survey of couples confirmed this. Those who prayed often together scored higher on every other aspect of marital happiness.[2]

If marriage were compared to a loaf of bread, spiritual togetherness would be the yeast. More than anything your spiritual oneness—or lack of it—may determine whether or not your marriage rises successfully or falls disappointingly flat.

In this book, we are not going to tell you that you absolutely can't have a good marriage if you are not spiritually compatible.

Many couples do. Nor will we guarantee you that if you pray together, you'll stay together. Many partners who do, don't. But we are saying that if both of you share the same faith you will profit greatly from worshiping, praying, and studying together. And we would like to explain how you can do this by drawing not only from our own experience but from that of many other couples as well: those who attended our seminars along with those who responded to a survey we conducted.

We describe various spiritual disciplines for two, devoting a chapter to each. And we face squarely the difficulties couples have relating spiritually and suggest ways to overcome them. This is not a book of spiritual devotions; it is a book about spiritual devotion. It is a holistic look at all aspects of being spiritually together, not just escaping to God for ten minutes a day. In fact, we believe these so-called "devotions" are not the key to spiritual oneness. Rather, what you need together is not a time with God, but a life with God, practicing His presence in many ways and times through an ordinary day.

Yet, we do suggest you have occasional devotional times. So, we've placed some at the end of Chapters Two through Six. Work your way through this book like you would one on the basics of tennis. Read how to do it, practice it, then play the game. We call the practice sessions TWO-GETHER TIMES avoiding the usual labels "Devotions" or "Quiet Time." The activities are broader than "Devotions," and they should be anything but quiet: We want you to interact energetically with each other as you do with God.

"Family devotions," and children aren't mentioned because we wanted to focus on the husband-wife relationship. Most married couples live many years longer without children in the home than they do with them. If all they do together includes and revolves around the kids, they could end up with little else between them. Therefore, even though they have a spiritual life with the children, they also need one that belongs just to the two of them. Our suggestions aim at that. But if you have kids, what you learn about spiritual togetherness will aptly apply to relating spiritually to them. And many of the TWO-GETHER TIMES could easily serve as family devotionals.

We suggest you read the book together and not hurry through it. Take bits of it at a time and discuss what's in them. Then, try to agree on what fits you best and how you can build it into you life. The TWO TALK questions at the end of each section will help you do this.

We estimate that if you meet two times each week for twenty minutes, you could work your way through the book in one year. This includes reading and discussing about your spiritual togetherness and practicing some of the TWO-GETHER TIMES.

Unlike a book of devotionals, you'll see this is not a book you'll use for a while, toss aside, and then look for another. Rather, it's designed to jump-start your spiritual oneness so that you can continue developing it on your own.

We have often said to each other "Why do things seem to go better when we are regularly in touch with God together?" We don't mean we necessarily have fewer problems or challenges; it just seems easier to face them, that life is OK, and so is our relationship.

The benefits of spiritual oneness are many. "We feel more united," wrote Joel, one of the husbands participating in our survey. Andrea responded: "Our paths become parallel instead of divergent or crossing each other." Steve stressed closeness: "Opportunities for sharing in faith our most fundamental issues . . . allow us a greater sense of intimacy than almost anything else in our marriage." We hope you'll discover for yourself, if you haven't already, what happens when you get spiritually two-gether.

CHAPTER ONE

Spiritually Two-gether

"For where two or three come
together in my name, there I am with them."
—Matthew 18:20

C hick and I were stuck. Once again we were discussing the same subject, feeling the same emotions, and at the same impasse. One year into marriage, we were trying to talk through a major marital problem. But, as in previous skirmishes, the intensity of emotions blocked our ideas somewhere between our brains and our vocal cords. I *thought* Chick didn't understand my point of view, and he was *sure* he didn't understand mine. We had said all we could bear to say. Our debate was foundering on the rocks, and we feared our marriage soon would be. There was one thing left to do.

"Let's pray," Chick said. Disheartened and frustrated, he took a few deep breaths, then prayed, "Lord, please help Ginger know how I am feeling." We both then said to God what we should have said to each other, after which we prayed together about our faltering relationship. We badly needed a counselor; we chose God.

And He graciously obliged us. Baring our souls we communicated with each other while we communed with him, a sort of "prayer therapy." Both of us are convinced that we would not be together today had we not been spiritually *two-gether* then. Each having come to Christ in our late teens a few years prior to our wedding, our experience of Him was fresh. Our dedication to Christ attracted each to the other. Our wedding gifts to each other were matching red leather-bound Bibles. From the very first we were heavily involved in ministry, in church activities, in studying the Bible, and in praying.

Yet, we aren't recommending prayer as a substitute for counseling, which, had we been wiser, we would have sought and no doubt benefitted from. God helps us through others. But we do claim that cultivating spiritual oneness can powerfully impact a marriage, as it did ours. For us, our spiritual bond was a saving bond.

It kept us united while the other personal ties—emotional, sensual, etc.—had time to develop. Our relationship to God gave us the integrity to confess our faults, grace to forgive them, and hope that we would overcome them. Essentially, we wove spirituality into the fabric of our total relationship.

This is why a number of veteran Christian counselors claim that *praying together* is the most stabilizing factor in marriage. "Pray together-stay together" is not an empty bumper sticker slogan.

This is not to say, however, that a good marriage is impossible for Christians who are married to non-Christians, or to Christians who have a partner who is indifferent to sharing spiritually. Certainly, lack of agreement on religious matters could disfigure a couple's marriage. Yet, they should do their best not to allow that to happen but should strengthen the bonds that tie them together: emotional, intellectual, sexual, and the like. And the Christian partner can use his or her own spiritual power and insight to make it the best marriage possible.

CONSIDER THE PERKS

However, two Christians in a marriage will benefit greatly by cultivating the spiritual side of their relationship. They will reap all of the blessings that come from being in touch with God, whether alone or with others: the joy of obedience, personal spiritual growth, the thrill of answered prayer. And they will receive much more; spirituality is very practical—for life and marriage.

Perk 1: Raises the level of your conversation and thought

Practicing spiritual disciplines together will elevate the level of your interaction and your thinking. Couples often complain that their dialogue has become superficial. One of my fellow professors with three children lamented how in-depth talk had seeped out of his relationship with his wife. Before they were married, they talked about their ideas, convictions, and feelings; now they talk about problems, food, and money. Once they discussed how they were going to change the world; now how they will make it through another busy day.

Taking time for talk of spiritual things, if only a few moments, will quickly rocket your conversation to a higher level, beyond the routine and above the mundane. There can be no higher thoughts than those about God. Think about godly things, urged Paul: "Whatever is true, whatever is noble, whatever is right, whatever is pure, whatever is lovely, whatever is admirable—if anything is excellent or praiseworthy" (Philippians 4: 8). Worshiping God together is a way to squeeze from our minds negative, destructive thoughts and elevate our conversation to higher levels and deeper intimacy.

Perk 2: Deepens your intimacy

Intimacy, which is the essence of married life, unfortunately is often in short supply. Too many relationships are deceptions. We hide our real self, fearing disclosure of who we really are. We hope it will be better in marriage, but often it isn't. Communication is not that simple, even for those who are deeply in love. "I live on an island and he lives on an island," complained one woman, "and neither of us can swim." Being with God together can help you build a bridge by having God provide the blueprint.

Most couples in our survey said things along the lines of: "We become more honest with each other about who we really are"; "It deepens our intimacy level." Drawing close to God together will bring you close to one another. You can't, for instance, pray with your spouse without communicating something of yourself to him or her. Emotions, ideas, yearnings—all of these will be exposed.

In fact, cultivating your spiritual relationship may even enhance your sex life. Years ago, in a *Redbook* magazine survey, religious women reported having better marital sex than other women. A more recent, extensive study of American couples discovered a relationship between their sex and prayer lives. Couples who prayed together often tended to be more sensual and romantic.

For decades, nationally known marriage counselor Charlie Shedd has been saying this, claiming that a wife is often turned on sexually by praying with her husband. Imagine, the sought after love potion turns out to be spiritual, not chemical.

Shedd claims this happens because sexuality and divinity are so closely linked. Perhaps he has a point, since some theologians claim humans are like God partly because they are male and female (Genesis 1:27). As God the Trinity is three in one, husband and wife are two in one; thus our capacity to relate in marriage as well as with others is because we are like God. Obviously, however, this relating is not merely sexual, since animals also do that, though they were not created in God's image.

Humans are different in that their relationship is personal and total—emotionally, intellectually, spiritually, and physically. Sex for them is not the joining of bodies but of persons. This is no doubt why the Bible describes it by the phrase "to know." Sex is a major form of human intimacy. By it, couples enhance their intimacy and also express the closeness they feel in other ways. Thus, in sex, animals *mate*, but humans *meet*. We love. In this way, we reflect the likeness of God, who is love. Sex for us may truly be "divine" because in it is an expression of deep personal intimacy.

Thus, if praying with her husband stirs a wife's hormones, it's because the act fosters a feeling of closeness with him. And that's what most women need to prepare them for physical intimacy as well as being a major goal of marriage.

Marriage can be an awesome merging with another human being. It is a lifelong reading of each other page by page. Each of us should be explorers of the other, reveling in excitement over the discovery of every new and intricate terrain. A marriage expert describes the thrill of such intimacy: "To explore the depths of someone else's personality is the most erotic thing a human being can do, and when that exploration is reinforced and facilitated by sexual lovemaking, the lovemaking becomes an episode in a grand adventure, taking on an intensity of pleasure that it would otherwise not have."[1]

Intimacy in marriage is one of the most sought after commodities in our day. Sharing spiritually is a major way to find it. Surely, if prime time television carried that message, we'd have more couples praying together.

Perk 3: Increases your compatibility

Spiritual togetherness can also make you more compatible. Couples in our survey made statements like: "We share the same value system"; "We have a sense of peace knowing we're heading through life in the same direction." Your loyalty to one another will spring from being more like-minded and sharing the same values, dreams, beliefs, and ideals.

Think of a triangle with God at the top angle and each of you at the bottom angles. The more each of you moves toward God and His will, the more you move toward each other. Total agreement is probably not possible, nor would it be desirable, since our differences enrich our relationship.

Think, too, of how much you can learn together. The wisdom you gain from Scripture and other sources will enable you to face life in harmony instead of at odds with one another.

So many of life's major issues are solved by a decision to seek first the Kingdom of God and then searching for what that means: what vocation to pursue, how you'll spend your money, what values you'll embrace, what church you'll attend, how to raise children (if you have them). God's truths will be regularly deposited in your joint intellectual bank account.

Perk 4: Strengthens your commitment to each other

Couples committed to God's will have a better chance of remaining committed to each other. They acknowledge that God makes the rules, including those that regulate marriage. Divorce for the wrong reason not only wrongs another person, as serious as that is, but it betrays God. This Jesus strongly emphasized when He said, "What God has joined together, let man not separate" (Matthew 19:6). Seen this way, marriage vows are more than a pledge to someone, they are a promise to God, adding a powerful reason to keep them.

Had we not put God first, our marriage would probably not have lasted. About four years into it, Ginger confessed to me that she had really wanted to leave me during the first two years. Not feeling that they were that bad, I was shocked. Explaining why she didn't, she said, "I don't believe in divorce, God doesn't believe in divorce, and my Aunt Vea doesn't believe in divorce." Social pressure, particularly from her aunt, with whom she had been quite close, kept her from splitting up with me. But it was also her desire to do God's will. Even though she believed divorce is sometimes justified, she didn't judge it was in our case. Many years later, we have a tremendous relationship, but it came not because we were instantly compatible but because we were intensely committed.

Perk 5: Gives you opportunity to express love

That married couples should love each other is common knowledge. That they can express that love by being spiritually together is not. I discovered this during a communicating exercise Ginger and I were doing a while ago. We listed the ways we shared our love to each other that meant the most to each of us. Ginger was sharing her list with me. Having been married for twenty-three years, I was not expecting any surprises. Was I wrong! The first item on her list was completely unexpected: "When you pray with me and show concern for my spiritual life."

I was shocked. I had never thought of my initiating our spiritual times as an act of love. To me it was a duty, something I was responsible to do. Seeing it as an act of love dramatically changed my attitude toward cultivating spiritual times with her. Since then, it's added a zest and a dimension that wasn't there before. Joining together spiritually may be one of the profoundest expressions of your love to one another.

Christian couples seem to be aware of this; or, at least, they seem to realize that it's good to have time as a couple alone with God. When surveyed, the great majority of them say so. Though they may worship, study, and pray together in church, they would like to do more of it privately at home.

However, this is one of those "Yes, but—" matters. Couples who say they would like to do this also say they find it difficult. Through the years, we've asked thousands of couples to list the obstacles to their spiritual oneness. Here's what they've told us, along with how we've suggested they deal with them.

TWO TALK

This chapter has identified the "perks" that a couple receive from relating together spiritually: Raises level of conversation and thought; Deepens your intimacy; Increases compatibility and commitment; and, Gives opportunity to express love. Each of you share which of these you would most gain by having a more consistent spiritual togetherness.

DEAL WITH THE OBSTACLES

Do these couples simply say, "the spirit is willing but the flesh is weak?" No, "not weak," but "week," they claim; there's not enough time in each one of them. Couples say the hands of the clock slice away a lot of what they would like to do together, including prayer and the like.

Face the time problem

Of course, it's not really the ticks of the clock that are to blame, but the activities we put between them. Busyness, couples maintain, is the number one obstacle, especially for those who have children in the home. When we've mentioned to people our writing a book on spiritual oneness, they inevitably ask, "Tell us how to find time for it."

First, keep in mind what being spiritual together really means. We sense that Christian couples too often think wrongly about spirituality by compartmentalizing life into secular and spiritual. Reading the Bible and praying together is neatly placed in the latter category. When asked about what their joint spiritual life is like, they say it's pretty scarce because they can't seem to sandwich so-called "devotions" into their busy schedules.

Part of the answer to this busyness problem lies in your trying to visualize all that you do as potentially spiritual. Being spiritual should not be confined to pious, ethereal escapades into the supernatural. It also can—and should be—a very down-to-earth experience that encompasses every daily activity. The kind of spirituality we are talking about is not what is associated with chanting hooded monks, praying cloistered nuns or hermits in scratchy wool shirts forever meditating. For them, drawing near to God required drawing away from ordinary life. Centuries ago, some sequestered themselves, the most extreme being "pillar saints," who lived on small platforms perched on poles. Others lived in cells, so small that they could neither stand up fully nor lie down at full length.

To them spiritual discipline was denying, ignoring, and starving their bodies in order to enlarge their souls. Their extreme discipline of their bodies earned them the title "athletes of God."[2]

Be assured from the beginning that spiritual athletics is not what this book is about. Spirituality is not an out-of-body experience. Those who tried to make it so had a warped idea of spirituality that sprung from adding to Christianity an idea of Greek philosophy: that the material world is evil and the spiritual is good. Biblically, of course, this is not true since God is the world's creator, who called all His creation "good."

By His incarnation Jesus demonstrated that our bodies and material things are not inherently evil. God, in the person of Jesus, became fully human. "The Word became flesh" (John 1:14). In this infusion of the divine into humanity, Jesus showed us that we can be spiritual in this life, in our bodies. God would not have incarnated Himself in a horse or an eagle. But, He could become a human because we were created in His image, making divinity and humanity compatible. Jesus taught us that we can be spiritual and human, that the godly can fish, eat bread, enjoy the company of friends, walk dusty roads, get their feet dirty, be hungry and thirsty, weep, enjoy a sunset, be caught in a rainstorm, be helped by a friend or be betrayed by one.

This does not mean that all that is in this life is good, since Jesus told us not to be of the world. John, too, commanded that we should not love the world nor the things that are in the world. Yet, Jesus and John were not referring to people, food, pleasure, enjoyable work, making love, having babies, and the like. Rather the world they warned us to detach ourselves from is the world of evil, the *cosmos*, which is the system ruled by Satan. That "world" is truly secular, because it leaves out God.

The Christian, to the contrary, attempts to bring God in, to desire His Kingdom come and will be done on earth. We need not escape this planet to be godly. Spirituality is not a flight of spiritual fantasy, an outer space fling or heavenly junket from life here and now.

To be spiritual is not to create a gap between the secular and sacred but to narrow it. Our book is designed to help you bridge that gap. We want you to see that a tree is not merely a tree but a creation of God; a peach not only a fruit but a gift of God; a spouse, not an evolved animal, but a person who reflects the image

of God; a job, not just work, but God's calling; etc. Being spiritual means seeing the divine dimension of earthly things. We want
you to believe that seeking first the kingdom of God includes talking with your husband as well as talking with God, that it involves
walking around the block with your child as a parent as well as
going around the world to reach others as a missionary. It means
studying your wife so that you can be more sensitive to her needs
as well as studying the Bible so that you can be more responsive
to God's will. It means injecting the divine into this world,
attempting to bring God's will to earth. There are wrongs to be
righted, injustices to be corrected, hatred to be confronted. To be
Christian is not to escape from life but to embrace and engage in
it. Informed by the perspective of God and armed with the power
of God, we are to attack life for the glory of God. Church history
shows this to be true. Godly people were the founders of orphan-
ages, hospitals, mental institutions, and among the foremost political and social reformers. Helping each other and others live
better lives here and now is being spiritual.

We want to help you make the secular more sacred and the
sacred more secular, to come to the place where making love is
truly spiritual and praying is very practical. Time, then, will be less
of a barrier to spiritual togetherness because that togetherness
embraces all of life and is not relegated to how many moments
you pray or read the Bible with one another.

Practice spiritual disciplines spontaneously

Busyness will also be less a problem if you practice spiritual disciplines spontaneously and informally. We do recommend your
setting aside some time for worship, prayer, study, and the like
(and we'll say a lot about this). But you can also intentionally do
these things anytime and anywhere. Insert them into your daily
life just as you do a kiss, hug, or laugh.

When God commanded parents to teach their children, he
stressed doing it this way. "Talk about them when you sit at home

and when you walk along the road, when you lie down and when you get up" (Deuteronomy 6:7). Couples, too, can inject conversation about values and spiritual matters into their daily routines. They can punctuate each day with praise and prayer and talk about God.

Couples we surveyed regularly did this. "We could be driving on a highway, see an accident and pray for the people involved." "When we get bad news, we both kneel and pray." "When we are overwhelmed with blessing we are amazed and praise God together." If you decide to take advantage of these unplanned moments and watch for them, you'll find scores of opportunities. You'll be amazed at how these bits and pieces of spiritual togetherness add up and satisfy that longing you have to be with God together and sprinkle a divine seasoning on your marriage.

Schedule some devotional times

Along with the spontaneous, put a time for spiritual activities into your schedule. Things often don't get into our lives unless they first of all get onto our calendars. One major reason couples give for not having devotions together is that no one takes responsibility for them. Choose a time and agree to remind each other about it but be realistic. Oftentimes couples are too ambitious. Engaged Christian couples often expect to spend hours every week studying the Bible together and praying. Months later, however, they confess that they discarded this ideal along with a lot of others that they had about married life. Plan for it to be brief. It makes it easier to commit to it, especially when you're tired. Besides, if you get engrossed and go longer, fine. Just don't count on it. There's no rule about how often. About this, Scripture is silent. Some couples schedule it daily; others, once or several times a week, designating, for example, Monday, Wednesday, and Friday, leaving other days for personal quiet time or devotions with the children. Too busy for even that? Well, how about once a month? Considering the benefits, do what you can. Don't fail to do something because you don't have time to do more.

Finding time will not be your only problem; you'll need to confront the other obstacles to spiritual togetherness that couples list, fear of intimacy being one of them.

TWO TALK

- Discuss how busyness possibly keeps you from being more spiritually together.

- Are the suggestions given in the previous section practical?

- Which of them especially impresses you as something workable for the two of you?

Deal with the fear of intimacy

Many Americans are embarrassed to speak about their personal prayer life, even with their spouses. In counseling couples, the Rev. Wade Rowatt, professor of pastoral care at Southern Baptist Theological Seminary in Louisville, finds that most spouses readily discuss their sex lives while "they struggle to talk about prayer."[3]

One of the major benefits of spiritual oneness, fostering intimacy, is also a hindrance to many couples. Typically, men will say something like: "When I pray, I get very honest with God. I can't do that in front of my wife." One man reported that it took four years of marriage before he could pray comfortably with his spouse.

The kind of self-disclosure fostered by prayer and Bible study can be threatening. Private thoughts and personal secrets are in danger if a couple begins discussing what a Bible text means or how it applies to life. Subjects may come up that are not often talked about. "Do you really believe in angels?" "Do you ever wonder if our prayers are answered?" "How do you feel about dying?"

We'll try to help you face any intimidation of practicing the spiritual disciplines. In appropriate places we offer some suggestions. And we've designed the TWO-GETHER TIMES sections to create different levels of intimacy so that you can select those that most fit your comfort zone.

Confront the threat of the spiritual giant

Differences in spiritual maturity can cause major discomfort over interacting spiritually. Though he knew he married an angel, he is threatened to find she is an archangel. She can quote whole Psalms when he still struggles to remember just how John 3:16 begins. And when they discuss theology, she mentions Calvin, Warfield, and Arminius as if they were members of the Dodger bullpen. Part of the problem is that it is downright embarrassing for him. When reading Scripture he stumbles over words like Amalekites, Ammishaddai, Uphaz, and Areopagus. She obligingly helps him with the pronunciation as if they were household words to her.

Whether it is the wife or the husband who is out in front spiritually doesn't seem to matter. Early in our marriage I turned Ginger off to serious spiritual discussions by my constant one-upmanship (emphasis on "man"). The chauvinistic robot in me often took over as I contradicted most of what she said and one-upped her with "but the Greek says." Not long after we were married she said to herself, "I won't talk to him about these things." Since then, I've talked to quite a few seminary students and pastors who have committed the same marital crime with the same results. Ginger's pretty much overcome the reluctance to express her opinion on spiritual issues, but it hasn't been easy. First, I had to become aware of how I had been putting her down and try to stop doing it.

Even differences in the way you pray can be a roadblock. A man said that his wife prays long, intelligent, intense prayers. When she does that with him, he simply falls asleep. Or else, he hangs in there and feels terribly inferior; he hasn't the fervor or the intelligence to compete with her. He knows they are not in a contest, but nonetheless, though he appreciates her brain and her spiritual vigor, he feels inadequate, like he's on the court with the spiritual equivalent of Michael Jordan.

Though a major problem, there are ways to handle this. Reading and discussing this book together should be a big help. It will serve to equalize your understanding and expectations of the spiritual disciplines. Also, *Spiritual Intimacy for Couples'* guidelines and TWO-GETHER TIMES sections are not tailored for spiritual giants.

Handle the pressure to change

Discussing these may pressure us to change. This too is threatening, especially when the change is closely related to our role as husband or wife. We know of men who, after hearing a sermon on marriage, drive home with their wife silently praying that she won't bring up some of the points the pastor made. Biblical passages may point out faults that you would rather not think about and certainly not discuss with your spouse. For example, if one of you has a problem with your temper, and it's a sore spot between you, a passage of Scripture dealing with anger could turn a spiritual discussion into a heated argument.

Discussing the Bible can be like opening up the proverbial "can of worms." Queazy about those squirmy topics, we would rather leave them in the can.

On the other hand, think of what we deny ourselves by keeping these things tucked away safely out of view: a chance to know each other better; a chance to deal with our problems; a chance to help each other grow in Christ. We are in a sort of dilemma: Spiritually relating can potentially make our relationship better, but we have to have a good enough relationship in order to relate on a spiritual plane. We'll suggest some ways to deal with this predicament as well as try to help you in each chapter and in the

TWO-GETHER TIMES to improve your overall relationship as you relate spiritually.

_____

TWO TALK

Two other obstacles to getting together spiritually are: fear of intimacy and spiritually related differences such as different levels of growth.

- Are any of these a problem to you?
- What could you do to face these problems?

_____

Settle the profitability issue

Many couples frankly admit that their so-called devotional times are not beneficial. Some say they are drab. "We quit having them because they were too dull," said one couple.

We suggest three ways to liven up your "Two-Times." First, make them relational. Couples sometimes make their times too much of a head trip. They share the ideas from the Bible and other sources, but they don't share themselves. Making the time more personal adds a warm, colorful dynamic. After all, being in touch with Him should not exclude our touching each other. Christ nurtures us through this personal contact. As you share yourself with each other, you will be sharing Christ who is within you.

Ask personal questions and spend time listening to each other. "What do you think about suffering? How do you feel about God's grace? How can we respond to this verse of Scripture?" This will brighten and enliven your devotions and make you look forward to meeting with each other as you meet with God. Many of the TWO-GETHER TIMES of this book will help you do that.

A second way to make the time beneficial is to keep your expectations clear. The key to doing spiritual things together successfully is determining why you are doing them and then plan accordingly. We believe the purpose is bound up in the word

"together." Don't expect from them what you can get from practicing the spiritual disciplines yourself. You can read the Bible
faster and better alone, for example, than the two of you can read
it out loud to each other. Your TWO-GETHER TIMES are not
designed to replace your individual times with God. Therefore,
don't study together in order to learn a lot about the Bible or
answer deep theological questions. If you expect to do that, you'll
probably be disappointed because that can be better done alone.
We believe that is why many couples feel their devotional times
aren't beneficial. They are doing them for the wrong reasons. In
the following chapters, we will try to describe those reasons and
base all our suggestions on them. We'll take just one example to
explain what we mean. We'll suggest that you should rarely study
a passage of Scripture together to determine the correct interpretation of every verse or resolve every issue the passage raises.
Sure, you may sometimes do this, but not as a rule. Rather, your
TWO-GETHER TIMES study should aim for other goals: to share
opinions about what is raised, to prompt you to praise, to give you
something to pray about or to discuss how a truth applies to your
lives.

When done for these reasons, the amount of time spent
becomes less of a factor; the quality, not quantity principle aptly
applies. What you are after are honest sharing of faith, sincere prayer,
and intimate worship. A few minutes of these can mean a lot.

Creativity will also keep your sessions from being routine and
tedious. In *Spiritual Intimacy for Couples* you will discover all sorts
of ways to bring God into your life and relationship. They are fun
and novel as well as serious and deeply meaningful.

If the couples we've talked to are typical, you should not
expect your spiritual journey together to be without its low points.
Most everyone say they, like baseball sluggers, have their slumps.
Circumstances, marital discord, or a partner in a spiritual funk can
sometimes bring a lull to your relating to God together. Try not
to be daunted by this by remembering the maxim: two steps for-

ward, one step backward. In the down times, hope for God to give you spiritual refreshment and renewal.

In the Preface, we said that spiritual oneness is to a marriage like yeast is to a loaf of bread; it will keep your marriage from falling flat. If you will give it some effort, we will show you how to keep the spiritual yeast in your marriage—and some spice, as well.

TWO TALK

- Do the suggestions for making your spiritual devotional times more profitable look promising to you? Why?

  In later sections of the book other obstacles to spiritual togetherness will be mentioned and dealt with.

- What hindrances do you have besides the ones mentioned in this chapter?

  One that is mentioned by many couples is that they don't know who should initiate their spiritual times.

- Is that a problem to you?

- Try to decide who should initiate these times and if both of you should feel free to do so.

CHAPTER TWO

Worshiping Two-gether

*"True worshipers will worship the Father in spirit and truth,
for they are the kind of worshipers the Father seeks."*
—John 4:23

Movie director Stephen Spielberg knows how to amaze an audience. Nowhere does he pack more astonishment into a movie than in a scene of *Close Encounters of the Third Kind.* Government agents and military personnel had set up an elaborate airstrip in a mountainous area, prepared for the expected landing of extraterrestrials. On alert, at night, dozens of them in and outside various buildings and trailers waited, scanning the skies.

Unknown to them, a man and woman, two of the film's leading characters, who had slipped past those guarding the site also waited, secretly peering down on the brilliantly lighted airstrip. Suddenly, a small ball of light streaked down from the sky and across the scene, like a sparkling comet, then another, and another, their darting back and forth suggesting that they were doing reconnaissance for the coming spaceship. Time elapsed and tension mounted. Then a flying saucer, not much bigger than a large airplane, came into view making the audience believe the flagship craft had arrived. But, apparently it hadn't, because this spaceship flew off, leaving behind an eerie silence of anticipation.

Then a deep buzzing, rumbling sound began. A low synthesizer tone. It grew increasingly louder, taxing the capacity of the theater's bass speakers as the edge of a giant, round spaceship suddenly appeared above the actors, its lights sparkling on its enormous underside. It slowly glided into the scene; only a part of its underbelly could be seen, indicating that its mass was many times larger than the airstrip created for its landing. As the hovering spaceship massively dwarfed everything on the ground, the camera shifted to the scientists and uniformed people who stared, eyes bulging, paralyzed, and openmouthed. The man and the woman on the mountain were awestruck, briefly glancing at each other to share their experience. With others in the theater, Ginger and I, too, were awestruck.

This is worship, in a way. Wonder—our capacity to be amazed—is the basis of worship. It can be generated by the sight of an immense, snowcapped mountain range or a glowing bronze sunset.

Sometimes it happens when we have a face-to-face meeting with celebrities, particularly those who have significantly distinguished themselves. Comedian Bob Hope's appearance produced this sensation among people at a hotel where Chick was speaking at sessions for Christian college students. Scheduled to speak at a charity dinner in the evening, Hope was spotted at various hotel locations during the day. Word of these sightings traveled fast through the group, electrifying the atmosphere as it did. Some scurried though the lobby and hallways hoping for a glimpse or an autograph. Those who were successful excitedly reported their encounters with others, which were then quickly circulated to still others. Some reported that they didn't know what to say to him when they were close enough to do so, a reaction that is known to be quite typical.

We can be awestruck before someone or something great: a sports car or a sports hero. This is how we should react toward God. Worship is a response of awe to an awesome God. For He is more splendid than a sunset, grander than any mountain range, more expansive than the starry sky. A vision of God should, above all, excite our capacity to admire and applaud.

There is something special about sharing with someone this

feeling of astonishment and excitement over something grandiose. Friends and lovers know this, since it's usually pictured in an assortment of romantic moments: sweethearts enchanted by a full moon, enthralled at an art gallery, rhapsodized by a symphony, or dazzled by a radiant sunrise. Aesthetic intimacy can be intense. No sharing, however, matches the sharing of the astonishment over the wonder, splendor, and majesty of God. You can do nothing more special for yourself and your relationship than worship God.

Ultimately, however, despite the perks we receive from worshiping, it should be done primarily for God, not for ourselves. A sign we saw in front of a church seemed to miss this point. "Make Sunday special; attend a church of your choice." Certainly, worshiping will add much to any day, as it will to a life and a marriage. Yet, ultimately and supremely, we worship because God is special. Worship is our vocation, as is true of all God's creation. Angels, stars, the sun and moon, lightning, hail, snow, clouds, stormy winds, fruit trees, wild animals, cattle, small creatures, birds, young and old, men and women—all are invited: "Let them praise the name of the LORD, for he commanded and they were created" (Psalm 148:5). Life is to be an act of worship. "Let us continually offer to God a sacrifice of praise" (Hebrews 13:15). Now, for some suggestions on how to do it.

TWO TALK

- How do you define worship?
- Do you agree that worship includes the idea of being in awe of something?

BE A COUPLE WITH AN ATTITUDE

Though worship can be emotional, it begins with an attitude. In a courtroom, there is no doubt about who is in charge. The one called "Your Honor" is to be treated as such. In the universe, God is number one. Worshipers acknowledge that there is nothing in the universe more worthy of honor than God. The English term *worship* conveys the biblical notion that to worship someone involves assigning worth to them and then treating them accordingly. Worship, then. is acknowledging God is special, then giving an appropriate reaction.

God's number one

God, of course, is remarkably unique. The word "holy," so often appearing in biblical scenes of worship, distinguishes Him. In a dramatic picture of God's throne in the Book of Revelation, those called "four beings" give God glory, honor, and thanks and never stop saying: "Holy, holy, holy is the Lord God Almighty, who was, and is, and is to come." Basically, the word means separate. But, angels around God's throne are not merely shouting; "Separate, Separate, Separate." What they are yelling is that God is distinct from everyone else: just, pure, righteous, powerful, mighty, majestic, noble, regal, everlasting, wonderful. God is special, in a classification by Himself, as above and beyond His creatures as the heavens are above the earth.

Thus, God has the clout, if we were to put it crassly, to insist that none should be honored above Him. And He does just that in the second of the Ten Commandments: "You shall have no other gods before me. You shall not make for yourself an idol in the form of anything in heaven above or on the earth beneath or in the waters below. You shall not bow down to them or worship them, for I, the LORD your God, am a jealous God" (Exodus 20:4-5) To put it in theological terms, God is "Wholly Other." To put it in plain terms: He's "Number One" where there is no number two.

Not being number one is just fine

When you worship together you remind each other that there is something greater than yourselves, that your lives are only part of a grander scheme of things. Otherwise, we place too much importance on our own goals, plans, and dreams, mistakenly thinking we are capable of achieving them, and wallowing in disappointment when we fail to do so.

Many marriages are destroyed by the way a husband or wife respond to life's disappointments. For example, couples who have a baby that is severely handicapped divorce at a higher than average rate. Losses, setbacks, conflicts, and crises can be accepted more readily when we believe that all we are and possess are of relative importance, that above all there is God.

Without such a picture of God, we can also put too much importance on each other. In one of his books, Christian psychologist Larry Crabb warns couples not to make idols of one another. His counseling experience has shown him that even though couples should expect marriage to meet certain needs, they often expect too much of their partners, demanding from them what only God can give such as happiness, fulfillment, or contentment. They end up disappointed with each other and disillusioned about marriage; and their partners are made to feel inadequate. Putting their trust in God, not their spouses, for these things will help make them more mature and content. This in tur will keep them from pressuring their partners to give what they are incapable of giving.

Worship involves putting God in His place, as Creator—and in the process, putting ourselves in our place, as His creatures. Worship evokes a humble recognition on our part of God's importance and the relative unimportance of everything and everyone else, including ourselves.

Something beyond a crisis

This eternal dimension, this recognition that something transcends our lives and our marriage, makes a major difference in how we face life's crises.

Chick felt this once in dramatic fashion in an exercise

designed to teach about grief. Participants were asked to write on separate slips of paper the five most important items (things or persons) in life. Then, we were asked to number them from one to five according to importance to us, number one being the most important. After this, we were to sit quietly and meditatively, and slowly, starting with number five, the least important, we were to tear each one up, fantasizing that it was thus being eliminated from reality.

My number one was God. As I tore up numbers 5 through 2, representing my career, Christian friends, Ginger and the children, I grew increasingly tearful and depressed even though it was a mere exercise. But, when I came to tearing up number one, pretending to annihilate God, I felt nothing but intense panic. Exactly why, I am not certain. But I interpreted it to mean that I can withstand any loss as long as I know God exists and that by His will we were created and have our being. It is by this that I can have the serenity to accept the things I cannot change.

Helping each other keep this attitude is the greatest support you can offer each other. When Job's wife failed to do this, she compounded the tragedy they faced. When they suddenly lost their children and wealth, "He fell to the ground in worship and said: 'Naked I came from my mother's womb, and naked I will depart. The LORD gave and the LORD has taken away; may the Name of the LORD be praised'" (Job 1:20-21). After Job's body was then struck with an excruciatingly painful illness, his wife bitterly advised: "Curse God and die." How lonely he must have felt as he replied, clinging to his faith in a gracious God: "Shall we accept good from God and not trouble?"

Job's wife failed him spiritually. Larry Crabb tells of a man who did the same to his wife. At the hospital a doctor came from the operating room to tell the woman that her four-year-old daughter had just died. Crabb explains: "In that moment she knew a terrible pain that penetrated to the core of her being. When she fell into her husband's arms, he coldly pushed her away and left the hospital. She was alone at a time when she needed to know that life still had purpose. When she needed to feel the love of someone close, her husband failed her."[1]

Contrast that to some of the couples who responded to our survey: "My fifty-year-old mother recently died unexpectantly. I would wake up in the middle of the night crying. My husband would hold me and we would pray together; then I could go back to sleep."

"Tracy was pregnant in July of this year and she developed some difficulties. We were naturally nervous about this so we prayed together and put the baby in the hands of God. Tracy suffered a miscarriage that same day. Although we were very sad about this, we were certain it was part of God's plan and that He is in control of the situation. It helped us because we could pray together; and together we felt what happened was God's will."

Putting God at the center, decenters us. Whenever a husband and wife bow their heads before God (or even more symbolically, kneel), they acknowledge that they alone are not capable of a meaningful life and are not captains of their souls nor masters of their fate.

This is the spirit of the lines a famous saint wrote on a bookmark:

Let nothing disturb you,
Nothing affright you.
All things pass.
God is unchanging.
Patience obtains all:
We need nothing else,
God alone suffices.[2]

TWO TALK

- How does the idea that God exists and that He is Lord of all affect your outlook on life?

RECOGNIZE YOUR UNWORTHINESS
AND DEAL WITH YOUR VULNERABILITY

Realizing God's worthiness should make us recognize our own unworthiness. One glimpse of the righteous God does that to you. Struck by the vision of God's holiness, Isaiah cried out: "'Woe is me,' I cried. 'I am ruined.' For I am a man of unclean lips, and I live among a people of unclean lips, and my eyes have seen the King, the LORD Almighty" (Isaiah 6:1-5).

A glance at God gives a glimpse of me

In this sense, worship is at the heart of being a Christian. We recognize that without Christ, we are so far from God that we can do nothing to bridge the gap, for sin has separated everyone from God. In the Old Testament, God was so unapproachable that animals had to be sacrificed to enable Priests to meet Him in the temple. God has provided a sacrifice for us.

To see God as Savior is to see ourselves unable; it means we must be vulnerable, defenseless apart from him. We recognize now that life must be lived by faith, not human ability. We take seriously the words of Jesus, "Without me, you can do nothing."

Seeing the dignity of dependence

Only God is independent; we are dependent. Worship requires humbling ourselves and admitting we need some higher power to make it in life. That's not too big a problem if you are all alone and no one is looking. But, that's sometimes tough to admit in the presence of others. There's a story of a man who had a traumatic experience while touring a tunnel called Hezekiah's tunnel in Israel. The few tourists in front of him with flashlights had moved ahead of him, leaving him wading in water in total darkness. He came to the place of near panic, overwhelmed by the feeling that he would drown. Yet, up to that point, he did not, could not, call for help to those who were ahead. A small native boy meeting him from behind, then showing him the way out spared him from the embarrassment of doing so.

Pride keeps us from asking for help, something that, in our culture, seems to be more difficult for men than women. Most wives know this and it often exasperates them, like when hubby won't stop the car and ask for directions when they are lost. We know of no scientific study that confirms this, but it's true—ask any woman. Men, too, may feel it's weak to stop and ask God for directions as well. In some sectors of society men are told: "Christianity is a crutch. Trust in God is a symbol of weakness." Often they are pressured to make it on their own, like real men do. Novels popular among American men feature superheros who have no need of the supernatural. A current novel lionized a man like this, one who was strong and crafty enough to endure terrible situations without once pleading for help from God.

Either men's or women's reluctance to appear weak may keep them from worshiping with their spouse. In the case of the man, it might not only be his discomfort with being vulnerable but with his wife's unease with his being so. A woman may rely on her husband's strength and be threatened when it isn't apparent. Many women, for example, are disturbed by seeing their husbands cry.

A man painfully crying out to God may not be a very pretty sight. Take a look: "I sink in the miry depths, where there is no foothold. I have come into the deep waters; the floods engulf me. I am worn out calling for help; my throat is parched" (Psalm 69:2). "I remembered you, O God, and I groaned; I mused, and my spirit grew faint. You kept my eyes from closing; I was too troubled to speak. . . . Will the Lord reject us forever? . . . Has his unfailing love vanished forever?" (Psalm 77:3, 4, 7, 8).

Yet, depending on your perspective, you could call this a magnificent picture. Someone has said that a man is never taller than when he is on his knees before God. Bible characters were often shaken, afraid, perplexed, and discouraged. They pled, wept, cried, moaned, sighed, and trembled before God. From a secular viewpoint, they were weaklings. From the Christian point of view, they were not. Weak and afraid before God, they were strong and courageous before others. One of them, the Apostle Paul, boasted of his dependence on Christ: "For when I am weak, then I am strong" (2 Corinthians 12:10).

Wives and husbands, if they are going to earnestly open their hearts before each other, need to give each other permission to appear weak. Praying in times of grief, confusion, or stress, they may lose control of their emotions; when they do, they need to be assured their partner approves. Or else, they need to decide that they must rule out such praying, agreeing to keep their worship together less personal. Whatever, it's important to come to terms with this and any other matters that may curb your practicing the disciplines together.

TWO TALK

- Is it hard for you to ask for help or to depend on someone else? Why?

RESPECT EACH OTHER

Some of those who study marriage claim that what makes good ones is what they call "positive regard." Couples need, above all, to respect each other as persons of worth. This is exactly what the Apostle Peter told husbands: "Be considerate as you live with your wives, and treat them with respect" (1 Peter 3:7).

Yet, someone's shortcomings and failures, like acid, can corrode the respect we have for him or her, especially in marriage where we depend so much on one another. Sometimes it takes just a few years for contempt to replace esteem.

Modern marriage is well-known as an arena for obscene mistreatment, physical abuse, verbal slander, painful neglect, and all sorts of disrespectful treatment.

Unworthy not worthless

Worshiping will help prevent this deterioration of respect for one another. We can't regularly revere God together without honoring each other because when we declare God's worth we establish ours. That we are unworthy does not mean we are not of worth since that is based on our being God's creation. This is precisely the argument James makes when he criticizes Christians for slandering others: "With the tongue we praise our Lord and Father, and with it we curse men, who have been made in God's likeness. Out of the same mouth come praise and cursing. My brothers, this should not be" (James 3:9).

Sometimes, based on the idea that Christians are to be crucified with Christ, some have taught that being spiritual means reducing ourselves to a totally worthless cipher. As a young man in the early years of ministry I thought this. Once, when teaching a group of college students in a meeting attended by a discerning Christian psychologist, I said, "Recognize you are nothing." After my talk this man, who was very large, came up and towered over me, shook his finger and blustered: "Don't you tell these students ever again that they are nothing." Then, he quoted Francis Schaeffer: "Man is sinful, but he is not junk." Wounded, I spent many hours pondering what he said, eventually concluding that he was absolutely right. We are not without value—simply because God created us. For this reason and to display His grace, God loved us and sent His son to die to save us.

In marriage, respect is basic. With it, couples will try to understand and be considerate of each other. Without respect, a partner may feel unloved. Tom's wife felt this way. "I only wish my husband would respond to me." Because he didn't know what to do with Sandy's feelings, he just froze up and ignored them. When she expressed them he didn't comment. His lack of involvement meant, "I don't know how to help you." But she heard, "I don't care that you are hurting." Of course that meant, "I don't care about you." It was difficult, for Sandy in addition to her hurt, was also trying to deal with her feelings about what she thought was Tom's lack of caring.[3]

Misunderstanding, or at least not trying to understand, amounts to rejection. And that's tragic. "The loneliest people in the world," observes one marriage expert, "are usually people who are frequently misunderstood. To be stuck with thoughts, feelings, and intentions that no one really knows about is an awful place to be stuck."[4] We have frequently heard wives say, "I don't share my feelings with my husband; he really doesn't care how I feel."

Respect means you can't ignore each other's feelings and needs. It says, "You're important" and translates into all sorts of positive expressions of concern: kindness, generosity, affirmation, support, and patience. Amazing, isn't it, that worshiping God together can have such practical implications and lay the foundation for a rich and satisfying relationship?

TWO TALK

- Do you think everyone should be respected because God created them?

SURRENDER TOGETHER

To those who truly worship, God not only makes the rules—like a referee—He directs the game—like a coach. Therefore, worship ultimately includes obedience and service. The most common Hebrew words for worship comes from the word that means servant. In God's covenant with Israel, service was the bottom line: "Fear the LORD your God, serve him only" (Deuteronomy 6: 13). Jesus displayed this notion when He battled Satan. After the devil took Him to a very high mountain to show Him the splendor of the world's kingdoms, he promised it all to Jesus if He would bow down and worship him. Jesus' blunt reply linked together service and worship: "Away from me, Satan. For it is written: Worship the Lord your God, and serve him only" (Matthew 4:10).

That to worship God is to serve Him explains why in the New Testament the major Greek word for worship can be translated by the word *service* as well. Thus, Paul writes: "I urge you, brothers, in view of God's mercy, to offer your bodies as living sacrifices holy and pleasing to God—*this is your spiritual act of worship*" (Romans 12:1).

The point is simply this: what you worship you will serve, and what you most serve is what you most worship. When your primary allegiance is to someone other than God, it is idolatry, for idolatry occurs, according to Paul, whenever people worship and serve created things rather than the Creator (Romans 1:25).

If marriage were a game, God would be the coach

Being dedicated to God gives couples an advantage in the game of marriage. When they, the two players, disagree—which they often will—they can turn to God, the coach, for a solution.

Granted, this will not make deciding simple, since knowing God's will is not always easy. But when you're both surrendered to God, it's easier to give in to one another since the solution to a conflict no longer lies in either "my will," or "your will," but in His will.

Living for Him, not for ourselves, adds an eternal dimension to every facet of life, including marriage. Said one husband, spiritual togetherness "has given us clear meaning and purpose in our marriage: to the glory of God."

Make the big "S"

There is no deeper issue in human life than its purpose, which determines so much, just as a destination does for an airliner. "Am I living for God?" is the question all Christians must ask. To worship is to acknowledge God as Lord over all, including myself, which translates into letting Him direct my life. Perhaps both of you have submitted yourself to God. If not, that shouldn't keep you from continuing to read this book and practice the disciplines it describes; we'll say more about that in a moment. But, first of all, what we've described as worship compels us to suggest you make Him Number One in your life because He is Number One in the universe. The first step for you may be to receive Christ as your Savior. Or, if you've done that but have still not made Him Lord of all, you may choose to do that right now. Perhaps, the two of you could jointly take your hands off your own life, as so many couples have done. In our early twenties, engaged to each other, Chick and I knelt before a couch in my family's living room and relinquished our lives to Christ. After forty-three years, our memory of that moment is as explicit as it is treasured, and the place sacred.

It's as if all the events of our lives are strung together and lead back to that spot. Our surrender to God was the beginning of our journey with God. That decision gave meaning to our shared life. It has since defined us, guided us, and made sense out of what we've done and what's been done to us.

That is not to say that we have easily and always obeyed God. We have frequently confessed our failure to do so. That we have had to surrender over and over again has not invalidated our initial surrender. The first one was necessary: the first, basic, most difficult step in our journey with Him. We look at it as the big "S." Since then, submissions to God here and there, now and then, are matters of a little "s." They are continual confirmations of the big "S."

Is there any reason why you cannot take such a step, if you haven't? Stop now and do it, creating your own memorable moment, with your own friend and lover, in you own sacred place.

If there are reasons why you won't do this, this may not mean that you can't have some joint spiritual journey together. All you need is a willingness to try to worship God by learning more about him and responding to what you learn. Maybe your spouse is totally surrendered and you're not, having made the big "S." Perhaps, you can make a little "s" by consenting to journey with him/her in worship, prayer, studying, etc., as best as you can. You'll follow along, observe, participate where you can and see where it leads you. That may make you both feel uneasy and vulnerable, but if you can handle that, then go along.

TWO TALK

- Is it difficult to surrender to God? Why?

- In what aspect of our lives is it most difficult to follow God's will?

PRAISE GOD TOGETHER

God doesn't demand we serve and worship Him simply because he has clout. Worship is also a response to His splendor, majesty and love. Dallas Willard in his book about spiritual disciplines summed it up well: "In worship we . . . dwell upon and express the greatness, beauty and goodness of God."[5] It is "in view of God's mercy," Paul asks us to offer our bodies as sacrifices (Romans 12:1).

Ought to or want to

Pondering the God who is love, celebrating His mercy and grace, will create in us the right incentive to serve Him. Too often, the Christian life is punctuated by *oughts*: having devotions, going to church, teaching a class, giving to missions, working at the homeless center—things we *have* to do. Worship, however, helps exchange the *have to*, to *want to*. Augustine put it bluntly, "Love God and do whatever you want." Our service is to be a loving response to a loving God, like a child helping his mother because of her love rather than obeying a baby-sitter because of her authority. A Christian is to be a slave without the attitude of one. Worship and serving should be so fused together that we cannot worship without serving nor serve without worshiping.

Ideally our lives should be a hymn of praise, as Psalmists so repeatedly demonstrated: "Praise the LORD, O my soul. I will praise the LORD all my life; I will sing praise to my God as long as I live" (Psalm 146:2).

Yet, maintaining an attitude of praise is not easy. Often we will not feel like praising God, especially because it's such an unselfish act. In Hebrews 12:15 it's called a sacrifice. There are things you can do as a couple to cultivate it.

Trust

Trusting the Spirit of God is essential to the practice of all the disciplines, yet Jesus especially singled out worshiping in the Spirit: "God is spirit and his worshipers must worship in spirit and in truth" (John 4:24).

"In spirit" doesn't mean spirited, as if worship is an emotional rush. We need not feel we have to be overcome with some supernatural visitation that makes us lose control, putting our worship on automatic. Nor does it mean that true worship only happens when God initiates it, moving in on us to make us feel like doing it. To worship "in spirit" means that we are to base it on the supernatural life Christians enjoy because Christ brings us into a relationship with God and fills us with the Holy Spirit. "In truth," refers to Christ, who is truth, the One who by His death opens the way for sinners to approach God.

Just do it

Because of this, we should take the initiative in worship. "Come near to God" (James 4:8). "Let us then approach the throne of grace with confidence" (Hebrews 4:16). Yet, as we do, we should trust the Holy Spirit to guide us and give us a sense of God's presence.

This means praising God even when we don't feel like it, for often our feelings will follow our actions. Ever lie beside a swimming pool watching others frolic in the water while you're content to soak in the sun? "Come on in," someone cries. "No, thank you. I don't feel like it," you reply. Aware at this point that you are in danger of being tossed in, you crankily and sluggishly stand on the edge and jump. Scarcely a few minutes later, you are happily splashing with the rest of them. Feelings sometimes follow action. To worship and practice other spiritual disciplines, we must "jump in." Inspiration does not always come to those who wait for it—but to those who go after it.

God promises a sense of His presence: "Come near to God and he will come near to you" (James 4:8). In our times together, let's expect to meet with God. Not that every TWO-GETHER TIME will be a winner that we'll be enraptured or flushed with excitement. Worship would be easy to do if every time we simply thought of God we would be overcome with this astonishment and wonder.

Sometimes this happens, particularly when God shows Himself by doing something unusual. Because of frequent miracles in the early church, "Everyone was filled with a sense of awe" (Acts 2:43). After Jesus walked on a stormy sea in the middle of the night and climbed into the disciples' boat, they "worshiped him" (Matthew 14:33). But God doesn't regularly do the unusual (if He did, it wouldn't be unusual) and we don't always feel things keenly. We are often distracted by work, moody, and tired. Sometimes our *excitement* button just doesn't work. We are dazzled by a wife's beauty one day, ho hum about it the next, thrilled by a husband's love one week, taking it for granted the next. We are the same with God. Yet, there are things we can do to put some zest in our worship.

Focus on God

The key to worship is this: focus on God, not yourself or your reactions. To have an emotional response to viewing the Grand Canyon, you don't concentrate on trying to be impressed; you look around, gaze sideways and up and down—you take it in and are then taken by it. To worship God we need to center our attention on Him. The greater, more accurate and clear our vision of Him the greater, the more intense and more genuine will be our response.

To get such a vision we must turn to God's revelation of Himself. Had He not disclosed Himself we could not find Him. Yet, He has given us many places to look for Him.

As revealed in Scripture

Scripture affords the most reliable and clear source of knowledge of God. The Bible is a record of God's revelation of Himself, given in many different ways, through people's visions and dreams, prophets' sayings, and events where God broke through into history. Later, Chapter Five will discuss your studying it together.

Now, we just want to stress one idea: You should have more than one reason for jointly looking at Scripture. Scripture will play a part in all the activities of your spiritual life. You should not open it always to get new information, to grasp another new truth, as important as that is. You should have many purposes for doing so, one of them being to prompt you to worship.

Reading any page can be a occasion for worship because every page says something about Him. You must decide to allow that to happen and not always get bogged down in a difficult passage or quibbling over an interpretation. Much of that is better done privately or in study groups, though you'll do it together occasionally.

Look for God in Scripture. See Him in the events: His power in rescuing His people from Egypt, His faithfulness in keeping His promise to send the Messiah, His concern in granting Hannah's prayer for a baby, etc. See Him in the analogies of Scripture: His desire to protect as a hen gathering her chickens under her wings; a father who gives gifts to his children; a sheperd who watches over his flock.

These events and figures of speech may evoke a more clear picture of God than abstractions used to describe Him such as just, kind, merciful, omnipotent, and the like. We have always had trouble with worship leaders who try to inspire us to worship by listing these abstract words. Let's praise Him for His holiness and His omnipotence. Not only is it hard to get a hold of the meaning of these words, but these words don't get a hold of us; at least, they don't seize our emotions. And we need to bring ourselves to feel rightly about Him as well as think correctly.

And for some of us this may be especially difficult. A woman once disclosed that she never felt God loved her, though several years at seminary studying Bible and theology had taught her that He did. She asked us if it might be related to the way her father had treated her."Often when I was in my early teens, when he was hopelessly drunk, he would keep me up to early morning hours shouting at me that I was the major problem with the family." Obviously she had transferred her feelings toward her father to the Heavenly Father; because she never felt his love she couldn't feel His. We suggested her considering other metaphors. Think of Him as a friend, shepherd, or other biblical image. Such stories and metaphors may teach us more about God than actual abstract words—holy, just, righteous, kind. Perhaps this is why Scripture employs so many of them and they cover the full range of His attributes. That He is just and will eventually judge the earth is cause for worship. One biblical writer puts this into a metaphor: "Let us be thankful, and so worship God acceptably with reverence and awe, for our God is a consuming fire" (Hebrews 12:28).

As a couple or individually, you will profit from meditating on these events and words. After choosing one of them, close your eyes and let your mind wander over and around it as you would leisurely walk through a colorful flower garden. Observe and absorb, take it in, and let the implications of these ideas sink deeply into your soul. If you do this together, after you have meditated, share together what you were thinking and feeling. Then, let worship follow: a song, prayer, or reading of a Psalm.

As revealed in Christ

There is no more concrete revelation of God than what we find in His Son, Jesus Christ. No miracle of God matches the incarnation. There are no more astonishing theological words than those of Jesus: "Anyone who has seen me has seen the Father" (John 14:9). In the New Testament we learn exactly what it is like to have God with us. There are graphic pictures of Him everywhere. Find them and let your imagination lead you to worship. What do you feel about a God who affectionately holds babies, who miraculously concocts choice wine for a wedding reception, scolds religious leaders for their hypocrisy? "No one has ever seen God." but Jesus "has made him known"(John 1:18). Seek God in what Jesus says, does, and what is said about Him.

Our greatest praise is for Jesus the Savior. A striking scene in the book of Revelation makes this clear. Elders, no doubt symbolically representing the church, fall down and worship something on the throne of God. Were we not used to this symbol of Christ, it would look rather macabre: It is a lamb, looking like it had been slaughtered, yet standing (5:6). The song the elders sing explains their reason for praise: "You are worthy to take the scroll and open its seals, because you were slain and with your blood you purchased men for God from every tribe and language and people and nation" (5:10). Then in a loud voice thousands of angels sing: "Worthy is the Lamb, who was slain, to receive power and wealth and wisdom and strength and honor and glory and praise" (5:12)!

A Christian's worship is most substantial when it is centered upon Jesus Christ and goes through him to God. When we worship, Willard says, "we fill our minds and hearts with wonder at Him—the detailed actions and words of His earthly life, His trial and death on the cross, His resurrection reality and his work as ascended intercessor."[6]

As revealed in natural revelation

Though Scripture and God's Son are the greatest and clearest, they are not the only revelations of God. God also discloses Himself in what theologians call natural revelation, which gives us four more places to look for Him.

God, like an artist, leaves His marks on what He creates. Just as an art expert can find something of Rembrandt in one of his portraits, so we can discover something of God in the universe. The Old Testament affirms this: "The heavens declare the glory of God; the skies proclaim the work of his hands. Day after day they pour forth speech; night after night they display knowledge" (Psalm 19:1-2). This revelation is available to anyone, says Paul: "For since the creation of the world God's invisible qualities—his eternal power and divine nature—have been clearly seen, being understood from what has been made" (Romans 1:21).

God's works can forcefully inspire worship. There may be some truth to the statement "I can worship God Sunday morning better on the golf course than I can in church" (well, just a little truth). Whether it's the scientist squinting into a microscope or a teenager peering into the evening sky, God's creation can produce a spirit of awe. A couple should take advantage of this.

Enraptured by a bronze sunset, a roaring wind, the regular rhythm of ocean waves, they can share what they see of God and briefly pray.

One couple spoke of their efforts to see God in creation: "Last Saturday we went to the Chicago botanical gardens. The effort was made to talk about the beauty and variety of God's creation."

They can also help each other see God in other people who are part of His creation and of natural revelation. Strange, we often overlook this, finding it much easier to see God in a mountain range than in our next-door neighbors. Yet, the revelation of God in people may be more important since they, not mountains, are created in the image of God.

That people have intelligence, feelings, and ability to relate to one another confirms that God, too, has these three capacities; yet outrageously greater.

If we are more intentional about it, these two revelations of God, in the world and in people, can by used to provoke us to intense emotional and meaningful worship. Too often, we think in terms of what should I be impressed with about God and thus worship Him rather than what am I impressed about. We sing

"Holy, Holy, Holy," in church and try to work ourselves up to praise, when in reality, the idea of God being holy really doesn't grip us, particularly if we're not sure what it means.

Why not start with what does impress you about God's creations and then go from there to Him? Are you awed by genius, perhaps that of a Mozart or a Bill Gates? Think about it. Discuss it with your spouse. When you listen to a Mozart piano concerto, move on and beyond to God, who gave him the talent to compose it. Think about how God is greater than Mozart and the music around His throne more majestic.

Or, if computers and their complexity excite you, if the whiz kid programmer, now billionaire businessman, Bill Gates, really turns on your floppies, transfer that passion to God. He is infinitely more complex than any mainframe, has limitless megabytes of memory, and is the one who gave Gates the mind to program MS DOS.

All around us, at any moment, are people and things to excite us to worship—if we open ourselves up to them, we also open up ourselves to God.

Husbands and wives may be able share even more intimate moments of worship with each other than they can with others. They can lie in bed after making love and praise God for creating lovemaking. They can see God in each other, His concern when our partner rubs our back because she senses we are weary, His comfort when one of us says, "I understand."

Mike Mason shows us how to see God in his wife, even in her nakedness. He compares her body to a shinning bright light he is unable to look at too long. "It is not like watching a flower or creeping up to spy on an animal in the wild. No, my wife's body is brighter and more fascinating than a flower, shier than any animal, and more breathtaking than a thousand sunsets. To me her body is the most awesome thing in creation." As Mason tries "to take in her wild, glorious beauty, so free and primal," he contemplates her creator. "In marriage," he says, "we learn that nakedness, like God Himself, is inexhaustibly contemplatible."[7]

As seen in his provision and providence

God is also revealed in the universe by His provision and providence. The first refers to His supplying what His creatures need; the second that He keeps the universe going and directs its events. Paul referred to these when trying to convey a notion of God to pagans who wanted to turn Paul into a god after they saw him heal a disabled man. "He has not left himself without testimony: he has shown kindness by giving you rain from heaven and crops in their seasons; he provides you with plenty of food and fills your hearts with joy." In another place, Paul says: "He himself gives all men life and breath and everything else. . . . For he is not far from each one of us. . . . For in him we live and move and have our being." Though there are earthquakes, tornados, and other natural disasters, the world does work under God's providential care. Usually, if you plant a tree, it grows; if you push the remote button, the TV normally comes on. There is order to this world of things, usually referred to as the laws of nature or Mother Nature, neither of which are biblical. Scripture claims God and not laws; the Heavenly Father, and not Mother Nature, keeps the earth operating.

During a week there will be scores of opportunities to worship the God who provides for you and rules in the affairs of your life, sometimes even in the things we so easily take for granted: a paycheck issued on time, a prescription that makes you well, a vacation that you badly need, an encouraging call from a friend, safety during a long trip. Take time to stop, look, and worship.

TWO TALK

- In your experience, which of the following most help you to see God: Scripture, Jesus, Creation, people, circumstances?

- From what you have read in this section about how God reveals Himself, how might you help yourself and each other see God and worship Him?

BE SPONTANEOUS AND USE CREATIVE
METHODS TO WORSHIP

Don't, however, relegate your worship to formal, planned times. Take advantage of the opportunities to be spontaneous, to praise God on the spot, at the moment of the realization of his greatness and goodness, when the wonder and surprise are fresh. Most of the couples we surveyed reported incidents similar to the following:

"We admire God's power during a thunderstorm and sometimes on a clear night, hold each other close while looking at the starry sky; we often get excited together at the first snowfall."

"We sing hymns and choruses in the car, and we stop and praise God after specific or miraculous answers to prayer."

Worship, too, can be a major part of your devotional times together, sometimes at the beginning. Some couples sing a hymn before studying or praying together. Often, your worship may be prompted by what you study, your praise following your study. Even an entire TWO-GETHER TIMES could be devoted to nothing but worship. This is the approach taken in the following TWO-GETHER TIMES, primarily because we've followed this pattern throughout the book, each chapter's devotional illustrating the subject of the chapter.

We strongly suggest your devotions be innovative with lots of variety. Christians throughout history have used their talents to worship God in dazzling displays of creativity: poetry, musical instruments, singing, story-telling, festivals. The Christian era produced a virtual explosion of creativity, employing the whole range of human arts: spectacular literature, music of all sorts, drama, paintings, sculptures, and architecture. The creative God inspires creativity in us, so worshiping Him need not be done in routine, drab, and colorless ways.

For this reason, you will discover that this book's devotionals are inventive and imaginative. Yet, they are not designed to call attention to themselves like stain glass windows. Rather, they are devised to be windows through which you can see the splendor of God and that splendor can shine on you.

Try some of them, after discussing this chapter together, using the following questions. The Father seeks worshipers.

TWO TALK

- So you think you could worship more spontaneously and informally? When? How?

- Would you be comfortable trying some innovative approaches to worship?

SUGGESTIONS FOR YOUR TWO-GETHER TIMES

Selecting

Though you might choose to do so, you need *not* complete all of the following TWO-GETHER TIMES in the order given here. Rather, first look over a few of them and choose one that fits your mood and with which you're comfortable. Then check it off after completing it.

After doing some of them, move on to the next chapter, saving others for later. If you do the same for each chapter, you will have an assortment of TWO-GETHER TIMES from each discipline left, letting you jump from one discipline to the other for the sake of variety.

Doing

Follow the instructions but feel free to let yourselves wander off the track. A verse read or a statement made could start you talking or a provoke a discussion not intended by the TWO-GETHER TIMES; that's fine; it may be just what you need.

No need to finish a TWO-GETHER TIMES; you may run out of time before you run out of instructions. No problem. If you choose, you can come back another time to do the rest.

TWO-GETHER
TIMES

- *Pondering God's Attributes*

    1. Look together at the following list of the attributes of
       God and their descriptions to determine which most
       impresses you about Him.

       Omnipresent: always present everywhere
       Omniscient: aware of everything that ever was or will be
       Eternal: not limited by time
       Spirit: bodiless
       Purposeful: has a plan for history and the universe
       All-powerful: can do anything consistent with His
          own being
       Sovereign: without violating the nature of things or
          infringing on human free agency, God acts in his-
          tory to do exactly what He wishes to do
       Transcendent: over and above and distinct from creation
       Immanent: permeates the world in creative power to
          sustain it
       Holy: distinct from all and untouched by any evil;
          righteous
       Loving: eternal giving and sharing of Himself
       Gracious: unmerited favor He gives to others
       Merciful: is tenderhearted toward the needy
       Just: rules creation righteously and fairly

    2. Discuss any thoughts or feelings you have about any of
       these attributes.

    3. Tell each other which impresses you most about God.
       Then explain what makes you feel that way.

    4. Pray sentence prayers to praise God for who He is.

- *Responding to the God of Splendor: Psalm 96*

  1. Wife should read first three verses out loud.

  2. When done, pick out the characteristic or characteristics about God described in those verses (for example, v. 3; great and worthy). List these.

  3. Then note what response is to be made to God (v. 1: sing, praise, etc.)

  4. Discuss any questions you may have about the meaning of terms.

  5. Husband should read next three verses.

  6. Then pick out the characteristics and responses as you did for the first three (Note: leave time for prayer at the end).

  7. Continue like this until you run out of verses or time.

  8. Pray sentence prayers responding to God as described.

- *Distinguishing God*

  1. Read aloud or each study silently Job 38: 1-21 in order to discuss the following questions:

     1). Why do you think God is asking Job these questions?
     2). What are the contrasts God is making between Himself and us humans?
     3). How does that make you feel about yourself?
     4). How does it make you feel about God?

  2. Pray briefly to God finishing the following incomplete sentence: "Lord, we praise You that You are different from us and that You are . . .

- *Getting a Vision of His Holiness*

  1. Read aloud Isaiah 6:1-5; while reading, try to imagine yourself seeing what Isaiah saw.

  2. Discuss: How would it make you feel if you had the same vision Isaiah did? What would your response have been? Would it have been like that of Isaiah? Why?

  3. Read verses 6-8. Discuss: How do you think Isaiah felt after he experienced what is described in these verses? Do you have any feelings that are similar to his?

  4. Pray together praising God for any thoughts or feelings that arose from your reading and discussion.

- *Worship in Action*

  1. Read aloud Isaiah 6:1-8. (Note: If you haven't done the previous TWO-GETHER TIMES, it would be best to do it before this one).

  2. This passage of Scripture describes the commission of Isaiah, the way God called him to special service. Discuss why you think Isaiah needed the experiences detailed in verses 1-6 before God asked him to serve Him.

  3. Discuss if there is anything in your mind that you think God might have you do that you haven't yet decided to do? (Perhaps you have a dream or idea of service you've never shared with your partner.)

  4. If so, discuss: How does what you have experienced spiritually prepare you for this? Discuss, too, how an experience like Isaiah's should make you feel about your present service for Him.

  5. Pray about your service or intention to serve as an act of worship.

- *Worshiping the Son*

  1. Read Matthew 14:22-33 aloud, each alternatively reading three verses at a time.

  2. Discuss what you think the scene in the boat looked like when they "worshiped him, saying, 'Truly you are the Song of God'"(v. 33).

  3. Discuss what they saw about Jesus that made them worship.

  4. Discuss what you think the disciples were feeling.

  5. Share with each other if you have ever had similar feelings about Jesus.

  6. Praise God for His Son. Instead of each of you praying a complete prayer, each pray a few sentences about what you are thinking and feeling, then the other prays for a brief time, followed by the other, etc.

- *From Creation to Creator: A Story*

  1. Read aloud the following story about a seventeenth-century monk named Brother Lawrence: "He had one of those striking experiences that I think we all have, whether we live in the country or in the city. One winter day he noticed a tree stripped of its leaves and reflected that before long leaves would appear anew, then flowers and then the fruit, and this consideration gave him so striking an idea of the Providence and might of God that it had never since been effaced from his soul and kindled in him so great a love for God that he was not able to say if it had at all increased during the forty-odd years which had since passed."[8]

2. Discuss why you think Brother Lawrence responded to the tree as he did.

3. Share with each other a similar experience if you have had one.

4. Each pray to worship Him as you discussed Him.

- *From Creation to Creator: An Exercise*

    1. In this chapter we described how we can see God in what He has created (just as Brother Lawrence did as described in the previous TIME TWO-GETHER). Using the following list to prompt you, think about what in God's creation most makes you think of Him. Share with each other what that is and what it makes you think of God.

        > Clouds and thunder and lightning
        > Flowers
        > Trees or plants
        > Children
        > Great people
        > The stars
        > The sky
        > Oceans, lakes or rivers
        > Animals
        > Food
        > Music

    2. Each pray worshipfully, telling God what you see of Him in His creation.

- *Praying with the Psalmist*

    This TWO-GETHER TIMES will introduce you to the practice of praying, using Scripture to prompt you. It is very effective, often stimulating you to pray about things you might not otherwise pray about. Simply read out loud two verses of Scripture and then stop and pray about what those verses have made you think and feel. Then, read aloud two more, then pray, etc. Though you'll be using Psalms in these TWO-GETHER TIMES, you can use nearly any passage of Scripture in this way.

1. One of you read aloud the first two verses of Psalm 34.

2. Meditate on these verses and then one or both of you pray briefly what they prompt you to think or feel.

3. Continue to read and pray alternately through verse 10.

- *Praying with the Psalmist*

  Before doing this TWO-GETHER TIMES, do the preceding one.

  1. One of you read aloud verses 11 an 12 of Psalm 34.

  2. Meditate on these verses and then one or both of you pray briefly what they prompt you to think or feel.

  3. Continue to read and pray alternately through verse 22.

- *Worshiping with Jude*

  1. Read aloud the following, which is the conclusion of Jude's New Testament book, where he offers praise to God as revealed in Jesus Christ.

     "To him who is able to keep you from falling and to present you before his glorious presence without fault and with great joy—to the only God our Savior be glory, majesty, power and authority, through Jesus Christ our Lord, before all ages, now and forevermore" (Jude 24-25).

2. Now, take each section, and read the commentary that follows. Discuss any questions, thoughts or feelings that you have as you read the commentary that follows.[9]

"To him who is able to keep you from falling"—though Jude has previously told us we must keep ourselves in the love of God (v. 21) here he uses a different word for keep, which really means "to guard," where the word in verse 21 has the idea of "to watch." There is a difference. We must watch that we stay close to the Lord, but only He can guard us so that we do not stumble.

"and to present you before his glorious presence without fault and with great joy"—God is going to set us up or make us stand before Him without any blame because of Christ's sacrifice for us. Without that we would shrink before Him. This will cause great "joy," a word particularly used of exalting at the heavenly banquet.

"to the only God our Savior"—God is one God. He is the one personal, holy, loving God who made the world, maintains it and redeems it through Jesus Christ.

"be glory"—splendor, like the radiance of light

"majesty"—respected as king

"power"—has control; the world is in His mighty Hands.

"authority"—the exclusive right to rule over all.

"through Jesus Christ our Lord, before all ages, now and forevermore!"—God's eternal radiance was crystallized in Jesus Christ; so was His majesty, the kingly greatness that suffers without complaint; so was His control, in the Lordship of Jesus; so was His authority over men, nature, and the demonic. Such is our God; such are His eternal qualities, unveiled in Christ.

3. Respond to what you have read and discussed in worshipful prayer.

- *Paraphrasing and Personalizing*

  This will introduce you to the practice of paraphrasing; it is a way of making a passage of Scripture meaningful and personal. The key to doing this is to let yourself go and write whatever comes into your mind, not writing to be accurate or to impress, but to be honest.

  1. Each of you read quickly to yourself verses 5-8 and 14-18 of Psalm 89 in order to choose at least two verses that you will rewrite in your own words. Try to pick some verses that seem to grab you as you read so that you would feel motivated to rewrite them.

  2. After choosing your verses, try writing them in your own words and expanding them with personal comments. Write until you have completed them or till you have no more time. The following paraphrase of the first verse of Psalm 89 will demonstrate the procedure. Note the specific personal comments I have inserted. Scripture: "I will sing of the LORD's great love forever; with my mouth I will make your faithfulness known through all generations."

  Paraphrase: "God, I am going to sing and speak of how You have loved me, how you brought me to yourself back in Johnstown, Pennsylvania when I was a teenager and made me feel You really cared and that you forgave me; I will also tell how You have been faithful since then, giving me a great wife, four children, and now grandchildren; how You've answered prayer countless times and picked us up when we were discouraged, especially over troubles our kids were going through; how we've both had opportunities to serve You and when we did You gave us the strength. I plan to tell others about this and to try to remind my children and other baby boomers of that and also explain it to our grandchildren and those of their generation."

3. Read your paraphrases to each other or exchange papers and read one another's.

4. If your paraphrase is in the form of a prayer, read it to God as a prayer. Or else, each of you pray worshipfully.

CHAPTER THREE

Celebrating Two-gether

"Let's have a feast and celebrate."
—Luke 15:23

Touring an old abandoned castle in Wales, we wondered aloud what it would have been like to live in rooms with cold stone walls and windows that were mere narrow slits. "Not as drab as you might think," explained our tour guide. "With tapestries on the walls and the huge bright warm fireplaces, the rooms would be quite cozy."

When we entered the castle chapel we quickly noted it had no hearth to warm and cheer it. Our guide explained that the chapels had no heat for the same reason they had no pews. Since suffering was part of worshiping, standing and shivering for long winter hours added to the effect. Their having tolerated worship confirmed that they were sincere and genuinely sorrowful for their sin.

In some places, the attitude that spiritual activities should be arduous and drab is still with us. And it's possible that couples feel the same way about their devotional times together—just one more chore to be done. Unconsciously, they dread them, putting them off just as they do other unpleasant things. The only way to do them is to force yourself, just as you do other things that are good for you but not necessarily enjoyable, like jogging or dieting.

This is wrong. True, time with God is serious business, and it can be arduous and not always fun. But Scripture never demands spiritual activities be routine, monotonous, and solemn. They should be joyful—perhaps not like a trip to Disneyland but not like a visit to the dentist, either.

It's true that God's people were sometimes asked to come before God sorrowfully, fasting and dressed in hairy clothes (sackcloth). They did this during times of mourning. And the prayers were often frantic and forlorn. In times of crisis they cried out: "How long, O LORD? Will you forget me forever? How long will you hide your face from me? How long must I wrestle with my thoughts and every day have sorrow in my heart?" (Psalm 13:1, 2). Yet, gladness was always not far away. "But I trust in your unfailing love; my heart rejoices in your salvation. I will sing to the LORD, for he has been good to me" (13:5, 6). Even the most mournful Psalms ended on an upbeat note.

This is also true of Israel's annual day of sorrow, the Day of Atonement. For twenty-four hours everyone was ordered to "deny" themselves (probably to fast) and join in a corporate confession of sin, while sacrifices were offered in the temple for national cleansing (Leviticus 23:26-32).

But eight days later, Israel was to lighten up. Using fruit tree branches and palm fronds, they were to construct temporary shelters, then camp out in them for a week of partying. "Celebrate this as a festival to the LORD for seven days each year," God said (Leviticus 23:33-43). Such feasts (and there were several of them each year) were fun and exciting, with ceremonial dancing, singing and noisy processions to the temple (Judges 21:21; Isaiah 30:29; Psalm 42:4). These were something to look forward to, cheerful interruptions of the laborious and routine schedules of ancient people. So were the other occasions for celebration: marriage, weaning of a baby, the visit of a guest or someone's birthday anniversary.

God's people ought to celebrate; we need to learn how to make merry before God, to have a carefree spirit of joyous festivity. Some Christians are not very good at doing that. We aren't always quick to see what God has done, instead, focusing on what He ought to do. During our seminary days of prayer, requests for prayer drastically outnumber reports of answered prayer, as is the case in nearly all the prayer meetings we've been in.

The same seems to be true of the prayer time of couples; it was with those who participated in our survey, few disclosing any intent to celebrate. Too often they used the words "drab," "dull" and "dry" to describe their spiritual times together. Could the absence of celebration be the cause of this? Would making them more happy make them happen more? We think the answer is decidedly "yes," so here are some suggestions for celebrating, not only during your TWO-GETHER TIMES but anytime.

TWO TALK

- Do you agree that there seems to be too little celebration in our spiritual activities in our churches and our homes?

HELP EACH OTHER SPOT THE GOOD

Put yourself on positive alert; help each other spy out the good. Some of us, more than others, will have to work at this because we have a good eye for the bad and a bad eye for the good. Generally, we find what we look for. Psychologists call this "selective perception." This is what causes Friday the 13th to still be a bad luck day in many people's minds. It's not that more accidents happen then, it's just that many people think they do simply because they are on the lookout for them more than on other days. Some of us are pessimists to the core, programmed to selectively see the bad every day. Behind every cloud we see another cloud and behind that a tornado. Contrast that with people like Oscar Hammerstein who wrote songs like, "Oh, What a Beautiful Morning." He was determined never to write a song that didn't have hope in it. His optimism didn't spring from being blind to trouble. He just made a decision to see the beauty of life as well as its ugliness.

Celebrators have to see good because thanksgiving is at the heart of celebration. To be thankful you have to have something to be thankful for; that requires watching for life's good. In fact, thanksgiving isn't just mouthing a few words of appreciation, it is an entire attitude toward life, a positive one.

Gratitude was a major mark of God's people in both the Old and New Testament periods. Thanksgiving was a major piece of Israel's annual festivals. They invited each other to praise, singing: "Let us come before him with thanksgiving and extol him with music and song" (Psalm 95:2, 6).

God asks Christians to be thankful, too. Said Paul: "Give thanks in all circumstances, for this is God's will for you in Christ Jesus" (1 Thessalonians 5:16-18). A positive posture toward life is so crucial to God because being negative is offensive to Him. This is why being thankless is associated with nonbelievers. Those without God often view life as something owed to them, taken for granted. Paul saw it as a major step in their moving away from God: "For although they knew God, they neither glorified him as God nor gave thanks to him, but their thinking became futile and their foolish hearts were darkened" (Romans 1:21).

When we are not thankful we complain and grumble about what has been handed to us. God doesn't like hearing this from His children anymore than parents like hearing it from theirs. Scripture says: "Do not grumble. . . . God is faithful" (1 Corinthians 10:10, 13).

Bellyaching about our lot is a sort of rebellion against God. Thankfulness is our way of submitting to God and His will. Paul wanted Christians to be "always giving thanks to God the Father for everything in the name of our Lord Jesus Christ" (Ephesians 5:20).

By this, Paul doesn't mean we should be grateful for everything as some Christians have suggested. For example, one woman argued with me that she had to eventually learn to be

thankful that her young daughter had been killed in an auto accident. All tragedies must eventually be settled in this way, she
insisted. As others, she was equating accepting with thanksgiving,
though the two are vastly different. Grief over adversity, loss, disaster, even crimes against us should eventually end in accepting
what happened. But, to thank God for these things trivializes evil,
amounting to a denial of its reality. Pantheists do this by believing
that God is equal to the sum total of the universe, including disease, hatred, ignorance, etc. that result in violence, accidents, and
death; thus, there is no evil. Christian Scientists deny evil by
proposing it only exists in the mind.

Evil exists, however, according to Scripture. And we should
not thank God for it. When Paul asked us to thank God for everything, he didn't mean all things, using the word the same way we
do in ordinary conversation. If I call to my wife after I hear her
come home after shopping at the supermarket, "Did you get
everything?" I mean everything she went for; I don't expect to see
truckloads outside of everything from the store's shelves. Paul
obviously meant we are to be thankful for everything that is
thankworthy.

Yet, in another passage, he does urge us to give thanks in all
circumstances (1 Thessalonians 5:16). We should always be on the
lookout for something to be thankful for. Even in tough times,
God's gifts are scattered about, and gratitude for these is always fit-
ting. Richard Foster aptly advises: "We should have a nose for the
gratuitous in life, following its scent, which is a fragrance, a per-
fume that goes undetected by the secular man."

Helping each other sniff out life's good things will do wonders for us psychologically and spirituality. Charlie Shedd explains
how he and his wife try to do this. Before going to sleep, they
often ask each other: "What's the best thing that happened to you
today?" To sort out the best, they have to recall all the good.

This trains them to cultivate a cheerful, optimistic approach to
life, highlighting the positive instead of dwelling on the negative.

An editor of a Christian magazine in a very funny Thanks-

giving article showed how, if we look, we could find something
for which to be thankful. Among other things, he listed:

- That there aren't twice as many Congressmen and half
  as many doctors.

- That grass doesn't grow through snow, necessitating
  winter mowing as well as shoveling.

- That teenagers ultimately will have children who will
  become teenagers.

- That women whose husbands take them for granted
  don't all scream at the same time.

- That no one can turn off the moon and stars.

- That I'm not a turkey.[1]

Because being thankful during bad times isn't easy, suggestions have been made on how to do it, some of which are quite
questionable. We try to avoid these. The first tells us to accept, and
even be grateful for, any human tragedy because good will eventually come from it. Based on the biblical promise that in "all
things God works for the good of those who love him" a Christian
should, when possible, try to visualize what good might come
from any personal calamity (Romans 8:28). For example, recognizing a teen's accidental death served to make other teens drive
more carefully is supposed to make it acceptable. This advice,
however, is not only untrue, it can be very distressing for anyone
who tries to practice it. Romans 8:28 does not guarantee that every
specific human disaster will result in some specific good. That
God works for good in all things means that in the sum total of all
history good will triumph. That is not the same as assuring us that
we will be able to see specific good coming from every bad situation, even though that's sometimes true. We've met many frustrated, even bitter, people because they were told to view some
awful circumstance in this way. One forty-year-old man is only
one of many examples we could give. "My mother died when I

was a child. People told me good would somehow come from it," he said. "I've accepted her death, but I've never seen any good results they said were supposed to be there."

Another suggested tactic to make us thankful in difficult times is to compare our situation with others, to see that it could be worse; thus, saying, "I fretted because I had no shoes until I met someone who had no feet." The flaw in this maneuver is obvious: It's selfishly insensitive to base our gratitude for a difficult circumstance on someone else's misery. We are to weep with those who weep, not be glad we're better off.

Torrents of appreciation for self and others should gush from a celebrating heart. So, too, should joy.

Couples need to selectively perceive the positive. Let's be like children looking under the Christmas tree for packages with our name on it. Let's watch for and notice life's gifts—every good and perfect one comes from God (James 1:17).

We stand a better chance of spotting them if we realize that God's gifts are not always miraculous. God's wonders involve ordinary things and often come in ordinary ways. Just as we learn to worship what we see of Him in natural revelation, we can learn to thank Him for what He does in so called natural ways.

Perhaps our failure to fully comprehend this is behind what so often happens at our prayer meetings: Our list of things to thank God for is often so short.

Perhaps, this happens because we see God in the supernatural and fail to see Him in the natural? "What has God done in the past week?" prompts little response because most of us don't have anything spectacular, unusual, or dramatic to report. So we are silent. Yet, there may be very ordinary yet very significant things that have occurred. A mother, for example, may have finally succeeded in potty training her child, which may be the most important thing that has happened to her in the past two years; yet, she doesn't mention it. Or, all of us had enough to eat or had warm houses to sleep in. Should we not celebrate these critical revisions, even though they're so common. Should we not praise God for the daily bread Jesus taught us to pray for?

Couples can help each other look at the brighter side of life by deliberately talking about it. They should try to make good news travel as fast as bad. Charlie Shedd's idea of simply asking each other what the best thing that occurred to them in a day is one way to foster it.

It helps if both, not just one of you, cultivate seeing the brighter side; otherwise you may get in the habit of being opposites: one the pessimist, the other the optimist. You get locked into a dependent pattern. The pessimist, when complaining about all the bad, relies on the optimist to cheer him up by cataloging all the good. As a result, the one of you who's negative, to keep sane, depends on the one of you who's positive. He complains, "It's going to rain today." She responds, "But the lawn needs it." "Yes, but we were going to eat lunch outside," he says. She replies, "We should be thankful we have a lunch to eat—anywhere." This pattern prevents the cynic from cheering up himself and thus keeps him stuck in negative city.

To help the pessimistic partner change, the positive one may have to stop being a hopeful voice for him. Ginger, who is the lighthearted one in our marriage, has done this to me, the skeptical one. In the early years of our relationship, I learned to depend on her countering my negative remarks with some positive ones. I didn't have to talk positively to myself because she was doing it for me. At one point, she became aware of this and she stopped playing that role. I would say something like, "It's a miserable day," and she would simply be silent. Her silence really impacted me. It was, first of all, a subtle rebuke, which I needed, a way of nonverbally saying, "I don't think much of your complaining." Secondly, when I didn't get a positive outlook from her, I had to look inside myself for one—or else, continue to steep in my own gloom.

After you've improved your scent for life's blessings, the next step in the discipline of celebration is simply this: just do it, anytime, anywhere.

TWO TALK

- In the past, where have you most found things to be thankful for?

- After reading this section, have you found new places to look?

CELEBRATE SPONTANEOUSLY

When you've spotted one of God's gifts, stop and thank Him for it. Be impulsive celebrators of God's surprises, like the father in Jesus parable: "Bring the fatted calf and kill it, and let us eat and make merry, for this my son . . . was lost, and he is found" (Luke 15:24).

This appeared to be the major element in the spiritual togetherness of the couples we surveyed. Many of them made statements such as: "When we're overwhelmed with blessing, we are amazed and praise God" or "We stop to thank God after specific and miraculous answers to prayer."

In addition to this, many couples deliberately tried to put an element of celebration in their scheduled devotional times, which is our next suggestion.

TWO TALK

- How and when have you both celebrated spontaneously?

- How and when could you do more of it?

MAKE CELEBRATION PART OF YOUR TWO-GETHER TIMES

Praise and thanks can be inserted anyplace in your devotional times, as one couple does: "We try to begin our prayer time (or end it) with a listing of praises, blessings, and that which we are thankful for, or that which is going well in our lives." At times, you may decide to devote the whole time to praise and thanksgiving. We have often done this, omitting prayer requests, reading, or study. One statement of thanks after another bathes us in refreshing thoughts of God's faithfulness. Our gratitude pleases God, and it certainly puts us in a pleasant mood, particularly when we've been feeling sorry for ourselves.

AIM FOR HONESTY

Deliberately being honest is one way to increase your capacity to celebrate, just as when you worship. Ask each other, "What are we truly thankful for?" not "What should we be thankful for?" Thanksgiving prayers are too often like the one in the joke about the couple on their wedding night. About to get into bed, the new bride stops her husband and says, "Aren't you going to pray?" The somewhat taken-aback young husband drops to his knees and says, "Dear Lord, for what we are about to receive, make us truly thankful. Amen."[2] Why not be thankful, instead of asking God to make you thankful?

To help students learn to be genuinely thankful at the start of a seminary class, I sometimes ask students to pray sentence prayers beginning with the phrase, "Lord, I feel good about . . . " I invite them to be honest, forgetting for a moment what they ought to be thankful for and thanking God for what they are. Maybe it's the fact that it's Friday or they're thankful they're eating out that night.

Little children know how to do this. "God, thank You for the wieners and the baked beans and the mustard and the buns and for Mommy and Daddy. I don't like the onions, though. Amen." We love to hear kids pray like this, and we believe God does, too. After all, He knows our hearts, and if our words don't match what's in them, they won't matter much to Him, since, unlike people who "look at the outward appearance," God "looks at the heart" (1 Samuel 16:7). Look deeply inside, find some imprisoned gratitude locked up there, and let it out. Let yourself go. God isn't impressed by the style of your prayers but their sincerity.

TWO TALK

- Are there any reasons why it's difficult for you to celebrate together?
- If so, what can you do to overcome them?

CULVTIVATE JOY

God wants celebrators who are joyful, sometimes hilariously exuberant.

To Israel, he said, "Be joyful at your Feast" (Deuteronomy 16:14). Nowhere in Scripture does God show exactly what He means by this more than in chapter eight of Nehemiah.

Once again back in their land after a long absence, hearing the Book of the Law read and explained to them, the people of Israel broke down and wept. Seemingly shocked by this, Nehemiah and the other religious leaders shouted to them: "This day is sacred to the LORD. Do not mourn or weep" (8:9). Nehemiah said, "Go and enjoy choice food and sweet drinks, and send some to those who have nothing prepared. This day is sacred to our Lord. Do not grieve, for the joy of the LORD is your strength" (8:9-10). Taking this advice to heart, the people went away to eat and drink, to send portions of food and to celebrate in a way they hadn't done for centuries (Nehemiah 8:12). "Their joy was very great" (8:17).

Christians, too, should be joyful. Though we aren't asked to observe Israel's festivals, we might take a lesson from them: that it's good to have some special festivities once in a while to add some cheer and hilarity to our lives. Celebrating is an intentional effort to inspire joy; something we should always be doing. Paul said: "Rejoice in the Lord always" (Philippians 4:4). And Jesus said, "These things have I spoken unto you that your joy may be

full" (John 15:11). Joy is so crucial to being a Christian that it
stands second in the list of fruit the Holy Spirit produces in our
lives, right after love.

Like being thankful, joy springs from noticing the good and
ferreting out evidence of God's working. Paul, for example, after
receiving some financial support from the Philippians writes: "I
rejoice greatly in the Lord that you at last have renewed your concern for me" (Philippians 4:10.). And joy may also include the
reverse: not just looking for the good, but overlooking the bad.
Celebrators perceive life with a sixth sense: a sense of humor. Not
taking themselves too seriously, they know how to make the best
of a bad situation, a priceless trait in marriage where so much can
go wrong.

Being joyful is not exactly the same as being happy. To be
happy denotes a feeling that springs from positive circumstances.
Joy is possible in bad times. Peter mentions how we may be joyful and sad at the same time, which sounds like a contradiction.
"In this [the coming salvation] you greatly rejoice though now for
a little while you may have had to suffer grief in all kinds of trials"
(1 Peter 1:6). Calvin says of this passage:

> It seems somewhat inconsistent when he says that the
> faithful, who exult with joy are at the same time sorrow-
> ful, for these are contrary feelings, but the faithful know
> by experience that those things can exist together much
> better than can be expressed by words. The faithful are
> not logs of wood, nor have they so divested themselves
> of human feelings as to be unaffected by sorrow, unafraid
> of danger, unhurt by poverty, and untouched by hard and
> unbearable persecutions. Hence they experience sorrow
> because of evils, but it is so mitigated by faith that they
> never cease at the same time to rejoice. Thus sorrow does
> not prevent their joy, but rather gives place to it. Though
> joy overcomes sorrow, yet it does not put an end to it,
> because it does not divest us of our humanity.[3]

It's easy to see how joy in the Lord can make us strong. It's an expression of confidence in God, of faith in His faithfulness. By it we confront life with vigor. Joy even makes you more physically robust and able to get over illnesses. Long ago a wise man observed: "A cheerful heart is good medicine" (Proverbs 17:22). Today, some scientific evidence suggests that the lighthearted have a better shot at staying healthy.

Your being joyful not only contributes to your well-being but also to those around you. Joy is a social virtue. To realize how true this is, observe just what being around a moody person can do to you. Grouchiness is contagious. So is joy. "A cheerful look brings joy to the heart" (Proverb 15:30). There's a married couple we love to be with. When we go back to our hometown we love to stay with them because they are so much fun. It's not that we do fun things, it's that the things we do are fun—whatever they are. They can make fun out of sitting around doing nothing. Each is like a stand-up comedian. Yet, they are not insensitively self-centered. Each also laughs at the other's jokes and ours just as enthusiastically as they tell theirs; and their routines are never insulting, hurtful, or embarrassing. And, when appropriate, they can be as serious as they are comical. They don't use humor to escape life but to face it, supported by their faith in Christ. Being a person who's fun is being one who's fun to be with.

Yet, our efforts to have fun are not attempts to forget our unhappiness, which is what much partying is all about. By celebrating we are not trying to distract ourselves from despair but to declare our faith. We rejoice because we believe God's promises, and those promises give us hope—to celebrate is to hope.

TWO TALK

- What circumstances or attitudes most keep you from being joyful?
- How could you deal with them?

DELIBERATELY REMEMBER
AND CELEBRATE PAST BLESSINGS

Apparently God wants us to celebrate what happened to us in the past, since He made this so clear to the nation of Israel.

And though Christians are not supposed to worship exactly like the Old Testament believers, we can practice in principle what they did. The church, like Israel, is a priesthood that should declare the praises of Him who called you out of darkness (1 Peter 2:9). Israel was told to recall past events and even to rehearse them by acting them out. So many of their festivals were reenactments of past times: the Passover, eating mutton just like families did on the evening of their rescue from Egyptian slavery; the Feast of Tabernacles, camping outside in flimsily temporary shelters, dramatizing the hardship of their trek across the desert after scurrying from Egypt.

Being hopeful is part of what it means to celebrate because hope makes thanksgiving and joy possible. Paul the Apostle confessed: "If only for this life we hope in Christ, we are to be pitied more than all men" (1 Corinthians 15:20). Peter maintained Christians could rejoice, even when suffering, because they had what he called a "living hope" (1 Peter 1:3).

At Israel's festivals when they praised God for His past saving acts, they also celebrated Gods eventual victory over sin. "Remember the wonders he has done," they were told because these pointed to God's power, love, and mercy which then inspired them to hope for the future (1 Chronicles 16:12). They were often told to build memorials, which, like the annual feasts, caused them to remember what God had done for them.

The writers of the Psalms often went back to the past to see the future, assuring themselves that God who had been with them would be with them. The distressed David, who lamented, "Will the Lord reject forever? Will he never show his favor again?" cheered himself by remembering "the deeds of the LORD" (Psalm 77:8, 11). In the middle of his mourning Israel's military defeat, the prophet Jeremiah said: "This I call to mind and therefore have

I hope: his compassions never fail. They are new every morning; great is your faithfulness" (Lamentations 3:21, 23). In a sense, God's people orient their future by setting their compasses to the past. Looking back to the past thankfully encourages us to look to the future hopefully.

There's something special about celebrating past events. Rejoicing in what God has done not only plunges us into positive thinking, it honors Him by remembering His works and His goodness. Chief among these are creation and salvation. By its annual Passover Feast, Israel constantly focused on God's rescuing them from slavery. Christians regularly, by their celebration of the Lord's supper, acknowledge their redemption from sin.

Any past blessing of God can be something to celebrate as well as increase our faith and hope, particularly in times of distress. When things are bad, we can then say to ourselves, "It's been worse, but God brought us through."

We have two suggestions to help you celebrate the past. One has to do with holidays, the other with rituals.

We suggest you plan how you can include some spiritual activities in your observation of major holidays and anniversaries: Christmas, Easter, Thanksgiving, birthdays, etc. Moments with God at these times can add a wonderful spiritual flavor to all the customary festivities: special food, colorful decorations, singing, joking, fun, and fellowship. And these things, whether done as a couple or with family or friends, can add festivity and joy to your relationship with God.

There are creative ways to do this, keeping with the special ways we usually observe these events. For example, during the Thanksgiving holiday after the traditional turkey meal, give each person a sheet of paper to list on it what they are most thankful for. Adults can help the children who need assistance. Collect them in a bowl, then let everyone pick a list, making sure it's not his own. Each one then reads the list he has picked. The group tries to guess who wrote it. Follow this by the reading of a passage of Scripture and then inviting people to pray.

For birthdays, invite people to pray sentence prayers, thanking God for the birthday boy or girl, right before singing "Happy Birthday" and lighting the cake's candles. In our family, we've shed a lot of happy tears doing this. As far as possible, try to match your spiritual activity with the purpose of the festivity. The sentence prayers at the birthday party are another way of affirming someone, which is the goal of the celebration.

Once inserted, these spiritual activities will easily become a tradition, an expected part of the annual celebrations.

Now, for a suggestion about rituals. Just as you add something spiritual to annual celebrations, you can put God into daily and weekly rituals. By rituals, we mean regular routines we've become accustomed to. For example, we get into a habitual sequence of activities related to getting up and going in the morning: coffee first, then bathroom activities, then breakfast, then dress (or is it breakfast, then dress?)—perhaps inject jogging or reading the newspaper, etc. Even our conversation becomes ritualized. "Good morning. Did you sleep well?" Rituals show up everywhere: saying good night or good-bye (kiss and hug, or just kiss or hug) eating meals, making love, etc.

Once these things become fixed in our lives, we expect them to happen and when they don't, we feel out of sorts. Think how you feel when you miss your morning coffee, lunch, dessert, or evening paper.

Intentionally designing rituals to include something spiritual can build the regular practice of the disciplines in your life.

It doesn't take a lot of effort, just a little imagination and planning. For instance, put couple devotions between coffee and dressing Mondays and Fridays; or before you say good night, say a prayer, or say one briefly in the morning while giving your good-bye hug. Our surveyed couples had a lot of ideas:

"Pray, holding hands, before meals."

"Pray in the car before we go on a trip."

"Thank God for safety after a trip."

"Discuss a sermon's impact after the Sunday service."

"Pray together out loud before we go to sleep."

"Listen to Christian music after getting up."

"Read Bible stories at mealtimes (with children)."

"Sing songs in the car (with children)."

Celebration is one of those familiar words that we don't pause to consider what it means, like the words chair or sink. So commonplace, we assume we agree on their definition. Yet, people enter marriage with different ideas about celebrating and, sooner or later, end up debating what it means and how to do it, particularly over practices related to the major holidays of Christmas, Easter, and Thanksgiving. Arguments about those things designed to lift our spirits—special foods, the Christmas tree, gift giving—end up dampening them. The source of these disagreements are, of course, lodged in our childhood family traditions and rituals. Of enormous sentimental value, we would like to continue to practice them, but they may be incompatible with our partner's; so, the conflict.

Compromise is one way to resolve it, each giving up some of his rituals and accepting some of the other's. Creativity is another: the two of you concocting your own rituals, starting your own traditions. With a little imagination, you can invent customs and establish habits that will saturate your lives with rich and meaningful celebration together.

TWO TALK

- How can we include celebration and worship in everyday rituals?

- How can we include these in holiday rituals?

CELEBRATE EACH OTHER

As married couples, you are in a position to celebrate something in a way that can't be done elsewhere: to praise God for each other. After all, in a sense each of you is God's gift to the other; you belong to one another. In the romantic Song of Solomon, the woman says as much: "I am my beloved and my beloved is mine."

To thank God for your partner not only praises Him, but it affirms your spouse. And affirmation is to a relationship what fertilizer is to a plant; marriages thrive on it. By a satisfying sex life, partners validate each other's masculinity and femininity. And in countless other ways they verbally or nonverbally accept or reject each other. If they are not careful, their messages will become more disapproving than approving.

After the honeymoon, some couples go from saying, "You are so wonderful," to "The problem with you is . . . "

Celebrating each other can help your spouse have a needed self-appreciation.

To be positive toward life we need to be thankful for ourselves. Otherwise, our own dissatisfaction with who we are acts as a filter, turning life into hues of gray and black. This is especially true during times of stress due to misfortune and misery when there appears to be little to celebrate. Then, self-affirmation is crucial. "Everything depends on whether, in the balance, we find our own existence a burden or an occasion for celebration."[4]

As we stressed in the last chapter, we are of worth because we are God's work. That we are "fearfully and wonderfully made" is basis enough for self-esteem (Psalm 139:14), for, as the Psalmist said, "All your works are wonderful" (v. 14).

Since we are sinful, self-esteem can't be based on our goodness or excellence. It is to be built on forgiveness, not perfection. Perfectionism, which seems to be one of our favorite neurosis, shatters any positive view we might otherwise have of ourselves. We may have learned this from a parent who did the same.

We have to face our perfectionism for what it is: pride. When we set our own standards we fashion ourselves as gods. This, according to the great theologian, Augustine, is the very root of all sin. Said the apostle Paul, we "exchanged the glory of the immortal God for images made to look like mortal man" (Romans 1:23). There is nothing human nature seeks more than to be flattered.

Instead of an inferiority complex, low self-esteem comes dressed in a superiority complex. So many of us seem to have problems with self-esteem; but, whenever we are tested, the great majority of us think we are more than average: we perceive ourselves as more intelligent and more sociable than our peers.[5]

David Meyers, professor of Hope College in Michigan puts it bluntly: "Most of us are not grovelling about with feelings that everyone else is better than we are." What causes the loss of self-esteem? We judge ourselves to be better than we are and feel badly that we are not. "Humility is often but a . . . trick whereby pride abases itself only to exalt itself later." A poor self-concept can come in handy: a useful technique for getting strokes from others. Humility does not consist of handsome people trying to believe they are ugly and clever people trying to believe they are fools. False modesty can lead to an ironic pride in one's better-than-average humility.

In Romans 12 the Apostle Paul gave the soundest advice to us about how to think about ourselves. "For by the grace given me I say to every one of you: Do not think of yourselves more highly than you ought, but rather think of yourself with sober judgment, in accordance with the measure of faith God has given you." Oddly, a low-self esteem can come from thinking too highly of ourselves. We have this big view of what we ought to be, and when we don't measure up, we don't feel right about ourselves.

Christian self-esteem isn't based on thinking there is nothing wrong with us. Becoming a Christian includes stripping away our defenses, taking an honest look at ourselves. That, in a sense, is a fatal blow to our self-respect, which is promptly restored through the cross of Jesus Christ.

We can see ourselves as sinners and still have a sense of our worth and God's love for us. I can respect my basic self and still not like some of the parts of what I am. Self-esteem realizes that I have strengths, too. I am not entirely sinful. I have potential. I can like some of what I find in myself. The bad doesn't wipe out what's right about me, nor cancel my potential and my worth. The same is true of others.

Why not also sing your spouse's praises to God? Hearing a partner thank God for you can be make you feel very special.

Sing her praises to others as well. When advising husbands to affirm their wives, Charlie Shedd somewhat jokingly suggested a man praise his wife to his mother-in-law. "She will, of course, tell your wife, who will be quite impressed."

Also, share in each other's victories. "Rejoice with those who rejoice," said Paul. Loneliness is hearing good news and having no one to share it with. Those who get excited over our success, victory, or good news affirm us. One of the greatest ways to love your spouse is to crawl inside her gladness and enjoy it with her.

Sharing in each other's happiness creates a powerful bond, the human equivalent of superglue. Failing to do so is intensely divisive, for ignoring each other's successes and triumphs is an acute form of rejection. Sometimes it happens because we are distracted by our own concerns and chronically self-centered. Sometimes it springs from jealousy and envy; we are uneasy over our partner's success. Obviously, we stop saying nice things about our partner because he or she has disappointed us. Whatever the reason, our relationship will continue to deteriorate if we fail to celebrate each other together.

TWO TALK

- How do you feel when you hear someone thank God for you?

- Are there ways you can improve your celebrating each other?

DEAL WITH HINDRANCES TO CELEBRATING

If we're going to celebrate, we may have to overcome some obstacles. In some respects, all of us are handicapped when it comes to celebration. Human nature being what it is, we are more apt to be thankless rather than thankful, depressed rather than happy. Yet, some of us may be more inclined than others to have a dark side that resists celebrating.

Adults who came from troubled families, for example, often have trouble having fun. They look forward to a picnic or a trip to Disney World, but when they get there they can't seem to enjoy themselves. Various explanations are given for this—one simply being guilt. Having been downtrodden by their parents or having blamed themselves for their bad homes, they feel too ashamed to feel good. Or else, their sadness like a shade tree blocks out life's sunlight. A parent's divorce, alcoholism, anger, etc. may foster depression in a child that stays with them into adulthood. A divorced woman discovered this when she asked her eight-year-old daughter how her mother's divorce had affected her:

> I remembered once he came home late and you got mad at him, but I really thought you got along just fine. . . . All the fun things we had done flashed right out my mind like when he gave me piggy-back rides and when we picked apples and when we drove fast down the roller-coaster road. . . . All I could think of was the bad times and all the bad times stayed in my mind, like when he got mad at me and when he had to go to the hospital with his back. The bad thoughts just wouldn't go away. My life sort of changed at that moment. Like I used to be always happy and suddenly I was sad.

For some, this depression stays with them into adulthood. Often it's most acute during times of celebration. Ironically, Christmas and other holidays supposed to make them happy make them sad because during childhood these celebrations were so painful.

When they become adults, too many of these children fail to deal with their painful pasts, choosing to forget them, instead. As a result, they cannot even celebrate the past because there's too much anguish there. But, confronting the negatives of the past can set them free. Once their feelings and attitudes toward the bitter events of the past is dealt with, they are free to see the good of the past, and they will be able to celebrate the good of today.

Another obstacle to celebration is dread. Essentially, a person is afraid to be happy today because something terrible might happen tomorrow. Many people grow up with this attitude. That it could result from a troubled family is easy to see because in these families, something bad is always possible, danger is lurking just around the corner: an auto accident or an alcoholic father or a beating from an angry parent. Life in these families is so unpredictable and scary, their children grow up afraid to celebrate.

Even superstition can oppose joy and thankfulness. Modern superstitions are rooted in non-Christian, pagan animistic religion. Animists believe demons are everywhere, behind every tree and bush and in rocks and animals. Because of the harm they can do, they are to be feared and placated by sacrificial offerings and various rituals. Celebrating any good fortune might prompt a demon to notice your happiness and try to undermine it. So, you rarely discuss the good things that happen to you, of if you do, you perform some ritual to protect yourself.

Though most moderns no longer practice formerly religious animism, many harbor superstitions based on it: not walking under a ladder or letting a black cat cross in front of you, or carrying around a lucky charm, etc. That many people still "knock on wood," after reporting something good that happened (to ward off any bad) shows there is still a lingering sense that celebrating today might bring calamity tomorrow. This puts a damper on celebration and runs counter to the thanksgiving, joy, and hope that God wants us to experience.

Perfectionism also gets in the way, since the perfectionist is never satisfied enough to celebrate, always wanting something more or better. A career army officer told Chick that when he received a new promotion in the military, his satisfaction lasted from the time he left the office of the commanding officer who gave him the news until he slammed the door in his own office. After that he started thinking about how he was going to get his next promotion.

Certainly God doesn't want us to become too satisfied, lazily and unproductively resting on our laurels. Yet, He does make it clear that He wants us to pause once in a while—to enjoy our blessings, to bask in our victories, to be grateful for good food, fun, friends, houses, trees, flowers, salvation, the Holy Spirit—for these are all His gifts. "Is anyone happy? Let him sing songs of praise" (James 5:13). God wants us to celebrate. Just do it.

TWO TALK

- What difficulties do you have that keep you from being joyful or having fun?

- How could you resolve any of these problems?

- How could you support each other in having more fun and being joyful?

TWO-GETHER TIMES

- *Noticing the Good*

   This TWO TIME is designed to help you notice the good in your life and give credit to God for it. "Every good and perfect gift is from above, coming down from the Father" (James 1:17).

   1. Each of you silently think about the past twenty-four hours to select the best thing that happened to you during that time.

2. Take turns sharing what that best thing was. If in the process you want to bring up other good things from that time period, fine.

3. Pray sentence prayers to praise God for the good that is in your life.

- *Thanking the Shepherd*

    1. Share for a few minutes about a favorite pet that you once cared for (turtle, pit bull, pig, and the like). Discuss what it's like to care for an animal, perhaps listing all the things you have to do. Tell each other how you felt doing so.

    2. Read Psalm 23 that sings about God's caring for us as a shepherd cares for sheep; as you read try to identify and list what that involves.

    3. Discuss which of these aspects of care you most appreciate right now.

    4. Discuss which of these elements of care you most need right now.

    5. Pray finishing the following sentences:

        God, Our Shepherd,
        * we especially thank you for caring for us by . . .*
        God, Our Shepherd,
        * we particularly need you to care for us by . . .*

- *Being Thankful*

    1. On your own, each of you make a list of the five items (things, people, circumstances, etc.) you are most thankful for. Don't let each other see your list.

    2. Now, try to guess the five items your partner has written

down and in the process disclose to each other what you have written. Discuss whatever comes to mind as you do this.

3. Using your lists as a guide, each of you pray, thanking God for these things.

- *Praising God with a Psalm of Your Own*

  1. Read Psalm 103, verses 1 and 2.

  2. Note that after the psalmist asks us not to forget all God's benefits, he begins to identify them, beginning with "who forgives all your sins" (v. 3).

  3. Beginning with verse 3 each of you on your own rewrite in your own words the verses that follow up to verse 14 (or as far as you get). As you paraphrase these verses, be specific and honest, writing down what immediately comes to your mind. For example, you may change "heals all your diseases," to "got me through surgery last year and gave me strength during the weeks of recovery." In other words, make it personal, noting what He has done and is doing in your life.

  4. Read your paraphrases to each other.

  5. One or both of you pray to thank God for what you have been reminded of.

- *Praising with Peter*

  1. Read aloud 1 Peter 1:3-9 in an attempt to identify what Peter is grateful to God for.

  2. Discuss these things.

  3. Share what you feel about these things.

    4. One or both of you pray to thank God for the blessings you have discussed.

- *Praising God for His Work in Your Life*

    1. Read Galatians 5:16-26.

    2. Looking closely at the traits called the fruit of the Spirit in verse 22, share with each other what two traits you most see in your partner.

    3. Now each of you share which trait you believe you need more of.

    4. Pray, praising God for the good traits you see in each other and then praying for the Holy Spirit's work in areas of weakness.

- *A Good Inventory*

    1. Using the following list as a guide, talk briefly about the good things that are associated with each area of life.

           Work
           Home life (as couple or family)
           Relatives
           Friends
           Neighborhood and nation
           Church

    2. Praise God for this good in your life, praying together any way that you choose.

- *Praising with Paul*

    1. Read Ephesians 1:5-14 with the intention of identifying what Paul praises God for.

2. List together, then discuss what Paul praises God for.

3. Tell what on the list you are most thankful for and what you have trouble being thankful for.

4. Each of you thank God for the items on the list for which you are most thankful.

- *Praising God for the Past*

    1. Choose a period of time in your marriage to think about. Your choice could be based on a place or a period of time. If you've been married for many years, you could select an early period of your marriage, if for only a few years, then the first year. Or else, you may choose a period of time you spent in a certain city.

    2. Discuss any good that happened to you during this time and/or people who contributed to your lives.

    3. Spend some time reminiscing about this period.

    4. Have a time of prayer to thank God for these events or people.

- *Praising God for the Past*

    1. As in the TWO-GETHER TIMES above, choose another period of your life and do the same as in that TWO-GETHER TIMES.

- *Praising for God's Help in the Past*

    1. Make a brief list of the times when God helped you in and through difficult times.

    2. Reminisce about these times.

3. Discuss whether any of these times of help might give you hope for His help with some problem or challenge today.

4. Spend some time in prayer praising Him for His intervention in your lives.

- *Sentence Praise*

  Simply spend your whole TWO-GETHER TIMES praying brief one or two sentence prayers for what you are thankful for. One of you start, then go back and forth and continue, stimulating one another to think about all that's in your life you can be grateful for.

- *Rejoicing with Those Who Rejoice*

  1. If you were to draw a picture that would represent how you feel when you are happy, what would it be? After thinking about it for a few moments, describe your pictures to each other.

  2. Think for a few minutes about what experiences makes you happy. Now, honestly tell each other what these are, noting which you share in common and giving your reaction to one another.

  3. Spend some time in prayer thanking God for happiness and for what causes it in your life.

CHAPTER FOUR

Praying Two-gether

*"I tell you that if two of you on earth agree about anything
you ask for, it will be done for you by my Father in heaven."*
—*Matthew 18:19*

If judged by the books people buy, praying is the most popular
spiritual activity. Werner Mark Linz, president of Crossroad, a
major publisher of serious religious books, reports, "Books on
prayer are our biggest sellers."[1]

"Prayer," writes one of these books' authors, "is a thirst." It's
a quest for meaning in life and a desire to commune with God.[2]
Another says: "Prayer. . . brings us into the deepest and highest
work of the human spirit."[3] A Christian must pray—and Paul says,
"Pray continually (1 Thessalonians 5:17). "It's life's electricity,"
says Dallas Willard "Prayer is the voltage that puts the surge into
our service and our engagement with the problems of the world."[4]
And if we are to believe the couples we surveyed, prayer puts a
surge into marriage. Consider how you can do it together.

SIMPLY TALK WITH GOD

Simply put, prayer is talking with God and there are many reasons
for doing so, just as there are for talking to a friend. In addition to
worshiping and thanking God, prayer is simply a way of socializing with God. It's intimate communion with God, and our soul

thirsts for it as a deer pants for water (Psalm 42:2). By it we sense His presence and increasingly know Him. Sometimes unspoken, the conversation is carried on deep inside us. Being moment by moment in a spirit of prayer is what Paul apparently meant by his command: "Pray continually" (1 Thessalonians 5:17).

As with other intimate relationships, true prayer can never be superficial since it requires exposing thoughts and feelings that are otherwise hidden in our soul's cellar.

It may be difficult for couples to pray this way together. Many wives and husbands say it is. Their level of intimacy with one another has not reached the level of intimacy they have with God. They just can't commune with Him while someone else is listening in. As a result, many couples choose not to pray together.

There is a better choice, however, and that is: use prayer to cultivate your closeness, yet decide not to expect or force a level of intimacy that is too uncomfortable. If you risk it, you may find what many of us have: that it is easier to open up than you might think. Praying can help you be more candid with each other. And, after all, Christians should be marked by honesty. "Speak the truth in love," and "put off falsehood" says Paul. (Ephesians 4:15, 25). Self-disclosure is so crucial to a married couple. It's necessary to solve conflicts since so much of what has to be dealt with lies inside us, in our feelings and inner thoughts.

Self-disclosure is also a profound expression of love, since the essence of love is giving and receiving. What is more loving than entrusting and accepting the most personal gift a person has to offer or receive, the inner self? But, marriage should not entirely deny us of privacy and personal identity. Being "one flesh" does not negate our individuality. The Hebrew word for "one" makes that clear since it denotes a composite oneness, more like two eggs in a pan, sunny-side up, not scrambled.

We must maintain our personal, individual integrity in marriage. To be close and growing closer, a couple need not feel compelled to share every thought, feeling, or secret, with total psychological nakedness being a goal. Nor should they aim to be impulsive about sharing themselves, thinking that true transparency requires going from the lung to the tongue, believing if you feel it, you ought to say it. Rather, as Ephesians 4:19 suggests, we should be careful about what we tell each other, saying what will build each other up. The rule should be, if you can't see any good in saying it, don't. At times, deliberately decide not to share what you're feeling, Christian psychologist Larry Crabb says. "A depressed husband should simply push his depression on the back burner when his wife is boiling from the pressure of three kids and a dirty house."[5]

Obviously, in our praying we can be too reserved and remain too distant, denying our partner necessary access to some of our inner thoughts. But, we may need to proceed slowly and patiently, realizing that intimacy is built on feelings of trust and acceptance, which take time to ripen. After decades of marriage, Ginger and I have shared things with each other that we once never thought was possible.

Praying freely with each other should be a goal, not a demand. The same is true of another form of prayer: confessing.

TWO TALK

- Do you agree that prayer is socializing with God?
- Do you find it easy or difficult to simply talk with God?

CAUTIOUSLY CONFESS

When Jesus included "Forgive us our debts" in His model prayer, He identified confession as a crucial function of praying (Matthew 6:12). "I'm sorry" is a powerful phrase. Said sincerely to someone, it can clear the air, relieve the hurt, and restore a fractured relationship. Spoken in earnest to God, it does the same. He has promised: "If we confess our sin, He is faithful and just and will forgive us our sins" (1 John 1:9).

Confession can also lead to change. "He . . . will forgive us our sins and purify us from all unrighteousness" (1 John 1:9). To purify may indicate that God will eventually remove the faults of those who keep on confessing them.

Richard Foster, in his acclaimed book on the spiritual disciplines, links praying to changing. "To pray is to change," he insists. God uses our conversation with him to transform us. In his presence, we become more aware of our shortcomings and are eventually motivated to do something about them. Spending time with God empowers us. This is why we can't spend time with God if we aren't willing to change; otherwise, we won't be able to pray for things to be different if we aren't open to the fact that they might be. Famous missionary William Carey wrote: "Prayer—secret, fervent, believing prayer—lies at the root of all personal godliness."

The same is true of confession; we won't genuinely confess sins we won't be willing to confront. Confession is an admission that a sin is a sin, a fault a fault, the Greek word meaning "to say the same thing." To confess to God a wrong you've done is essentially to saying to Him, "I am saying the same thing about this as You do." It is seeing things from God's point of view. God says, "It's sin." By confessing, we say, "Right."

Confession is an affirmation of the way things are and the way they ought to be. By admitting what is wrong, we are acknowledging what is right. This is one of the reasons it is so necessary. By saying to God, I fall short of the ideal, I uphold the ideal. I remind myself of how I ought to change. For this reason, we should never give up confessing a sin, even if we have repeatedly failed to overcome it, and we feel frustrated and defeated. For as soon as we stop labeling it wrong, we think of it as right. By confessing and praying we continually remind ourselves of God's point of view.

Confession, even though it is so personal, can play a role in a couple's prayer life. In our survey, when we asked couples if they felt free to confess sins before one another, one husband replied, "Yes. We keep each other accountable and try to keep short accounts." Another reported, "I feel free to confess sins in front of my spouse. I think she feels likewise, but we don't do this regularly."

Another husband, like some others, was reluctant to confess everything. "I feel very free to confess some sins, especially ones of character, with my spouse. Unfortunately this occurs primarily in context of sins outside the home, and not often enough where she may be the victim" Another said, "The ones I have difficulty confessing relate to purity or impure thoughts."

Obviously, sharing in this area of the spiritual life can be troublesome. Some things stand in the way and they may need to be brought into the open, discussed, and dealt with.

For one thing, if we pray about our shortcomings in our partner's presence we risk looking like a hypocrite. Some of our personal faults are difficult to overcome. We may confess our anger and yet still be our own cranky self. We may pray for patience while continuing to be irritable and testy. Our spouse may be thinking, "Stop praying, and do something about it." Or, even if he/she isn't thinking it, we may imagine he/she is.

Our lives don't always live up to the level of our prayers, as one writer ideally suggests they should: "We live the way we pray and we pray the way we live."[6] Scripture teaches otherwise: that we should be praying beyond and above the level of our living. We pray for God's complete will to be done in our lives even though it's not. Our prayers express our dreams, desires, and hope for what ought to be. In them, our reach should exceed our grasp.

However, we must also expect that any confessions in our presence, if done at all, be honest ones, expressing a desire to change. We must not permit ourselves to use prayer and confession as an excuse for remaining the way we are. A wife who regularly verbally abuses her husband or a husband who habitually neglects his wife may feel it is enough to say "I'm sorry," while doing nothing to correct this behavior. Obsessed or addicted persons are the most apt to do this. They need a dose of tough love. Their partners must insist they match their confession of a problem with some effort to solve it—consenting to counseling or joining a support group or the like.

Yet, normally couples will have to permit each other's conduct to fall short of their confessions, while they each try to measure up to them. As Christ accepts them, blemishes and all, so they will need to accept each other.

They also need to be open to a joint confession. Times of failure together need to be confessed together. Jesus suggested this in the Lord's prayer with its plural pronouns, "Forgive us our debts." And after failing one another, you will find nothing heals the hurt of being injured by your partner as does hearing him or her confess that wrong to God.

The next type of prayer will be more common and comfortable: prayer as petition.

TWO TALK

- When do you think it is appropriate to confess your faults to God before each other?

REQUEST AND RELY

Prayer as asking God for favors is one of the oldest and most human forms of prayer. Linguistically, the root words for prayer is from the Latin, *precarious* "obtained by begging." "Ask and it will be given you," said Jesus.

In fact, Scripture gives the impression Christians should petition God about everything: "In everything by prayer and petition, with thanksgiving present your requests to God" (Philippians 4:6). John Wesley taught that "God does nothing but in answer to prayer," though thankfully, this is probably not true. Yet, we are repeatedly told to pray regularly for what we need: daily, not weekly, bread, said Jesus. And the Apostle James scolds, "You do not have because you do not ask." What if we looked at prayer like we do shopping, having groceries tomorrow depending on one of us getting to the store today?

Apparently nothing should be excluded from prayer, even small matters. Perhaps all of us have felt reluctant to pray about something that was bothersome but rather insignificant. A woman once said as much to a prominent Bible teacher, claiming she only felt free to pray about life's big things. He answered, "Can you really bring anything to God that is big to Him?"

God even asks us to pray for those things he has already promised. "Nothing is promised to be expected from the Lord, which we are not also bidden to ask of him in prayer,"[7] observed John Calvin. He compared prayer to digging up treasure, arguing that it would be strange for a person to neglect riches, buried and hidden in the earth, after they had been pointed out to him. Prayer is the way to get to them.

The things Jesus taught us to pray for in the Lord's prayer are the things that tend to concern us most: justice and peace; that God's kingdom and will be done on earth as it is in heaven; physical needs (daily bread being a figure of speech that refers to food for the day); guidance (that we not be brought into temptation or be put to the test, either by trials or by Satan); deliverance from evil.

And He told us to ask persistently. Prayer, explained Jesus, is like going to a friend's house at midnight to borrow some bread because you've had a traveler suddenly pop in on you, and you have nothing in the house to eat. Through the door your sleepy friend yells, "Don't bother me; we're all bedded down for the night." Yet, says Jesus, "I tell you, though he will not get up and give him the bread because he is his friend, yet because of the man's boldness he will get up and give him as much as he needs." So, when it comes to prayer, "Ask and it will be given to you; seek and you will find; knock and the door will be opened to you" (Luke 11:5-10).

Apparently, Jesus isn't implying God is like a sleeping friend who only responds when we bug him enough. Actually, He's trying to say the opposite: God is eager to give, much like a father responds to his kids. "Which of you, if his son asks for bread, will give him a stone? If you, then, though you are evil, know how to give good gifts to your children, how much more will your Father in heaven give good gifts to those who asks?" (Matthew 7:7-11). What He apparently means by His example of persistence is that we should pray with feeling and that we should keep it up, sometimes hard and long. But, we shouldn't think that we can get God to answer by beating on His ears with a barrage of words. In fact, He cautions us not to confuse persistence with repetition: "And when you pray, do not keep on babbling like pagans, for they think they will be heard because of their many words. Do not be like them, for your Father knows what you need before you ask him" (Matthew 6:7-8).

Probably all of us, at one time or another, has questioned the value of prayer. Certain objections to praying need to be dealt with. One has to do with the sovereignty of God, arguing, "If God foreknows everything and has planned it all, how can prayer make any difference?" This objection is also related to the matter of free will: "If we choose to act in a certain way today, how can God fit that into the plan He made in the past?" These are tough questions that we can't fully answer. Yet, they shouldn't keep us from praying since God has told us that prayers really do matter. And we can believe since God knows the future, He included in His grand scheme of things our prayers and His response. So that we can truly say God does really answer prayer and that prayer is not insignificant; it's crucial that we pray.

Another objection springs from the fact that God is all knowing. "If God already knows what we need and outclasses even the most generous dad, why do we have to ask Him at all?" The answer to this is simply that informing God is not the only reason for praying. Prayer is more than a spiritual shopping trip. A look at the reasons for praying, which we will now do, should give us additional reasons to pray, not only alone, but together.

To see the faithfulness of God

John Calvin insisted God asks us to pray not for His sake, but for ours. Praying enables us to recognize all we desire and need comes from God. When we receive some gift, we know that God is the giver because He is the one we asked, as did the Psalmist. "God has surely listened and heard my voice in prayer. Praise be to God" (Psalm 66:19). Having to wait for an answer makes us more thankful when it finally comes. If you join together in prayer, you'll more likely join together in praise. "One thing we have found to be true is the amazing faithfulness of God in giving us direction for our future," a husband wrote. "We look at how He has always provided us both with a certain amount of certainty when it comes to His will for our lives."

To testify of His faithfulness to others

That we pray and God answers is a way God brings glory to Himself. After the Psalmist said God heard his prayer, he shouted, "Come and listen, all you who fear God; let me tell you what he has done for me" (Psalm 66:19). Couples who pray together can be a witness to others of God's grace. "Let the afflicted hear and rejoice. . . . This poor man called, and the LORD heard him; he saved him out of all his troubles" (Psalm 34:6). When our children were troubled or rebellious, we were encouraged to continue praying for them by other parents who had seen God answer prayer in their children's lives in similar situations. Now, having seen for ourselves the effects of prayer in our teen's lives, we are able to inspire other parents to trust God for their children.

To foster our dependence and excercise our faith

Having to ask reminds us continually of our dependence on God and keeps us alert for His answers. When God promised Elijah that it would rain, Elijah still prayed for it (1 Kings 18:42). Calvin speculates that he did so "because he knew it was his duty, lest his faith be sleepy or sluggish." Prayer offers a chance to believe. Praying strengthens our faith as exercise does our bodies, increasing our spiritual pulse rate and toughening our inner heart.

Any petition you make to God is an exercise in faith, since it is to be offered in faith. "Have faith in God. . . ." said Jesus, "Whatever you ask for in prayer, believe that you have received it, and it will be yours" (Mark 11:22, 24). George Mueller, famous for his faith, said that the most important part of prayer was the fifteen minutes after he said, "Amen."

Essentially he was saying the same thing as Judson Cornwall:

> If prayer's purpose is to get an answer from God, then we should pray expecting an answer. There is no room for vagueness in our praying. If we have a petition, it should be stated clearly, right to the point, and given in an expectant tone . . . people would never be so vague in dealing with a banker.[8]

Petitioning God together will keep both of you peering toward Heaven, waiting for God to amaze you. You'll share the most exciting journey of all, the venture of faith.

To deal with anxiety

When the Apostle Peter advised suffering Christians to cast all their anxiety upon God, he apparently wasn't referring only to their problems but also to their emotions. Toss your feeling of anxiety on God, he said, "because he cares for you" (1 Peter 5:7). Prayer gives us a chance to get things off our chest; it's therapeutic and not always a search for an answer, but for an outlet.[9] The language of prayer includes agonizing cries from the depths of our souls: "I do believe, help me overcome my unbelief" (Mark 9:24); "My heart is in anguish within me. . . . Fear and trembling have beset me" (Psalm 55:5, 6). Sometimes we pray to change ourselves, not our circumstances. Knowing God hears our moans, notices our misery, and considers our troubled thoughts, soothes some of our pain and fear. A Marxist philosopher asked Johann Baptist Metz how Christians can still pray after the Holocaust, when God permitted millions of Jews to be unmercifully slaughtered. Metz replied that the only answer was that "We can and should pray after Auschwitz because even in Auschwitz, in the hell of Auschwitz, they prayed." Prayer is not always about answers . . . but about impassioned questions.[10]

God knows our need to ventilate our anxiety just as we know children need to talk to us about theirs. In search of comfort, terrorized by a roaring thunderstorm, they crawl into our bed at 2 A.M. and murmur, "Scared." Or en route to Grandma's house, they ask repeatedly, "Are we there yet? How long will it be?" What kind of parent shrieks "Go back to bed!" or "Will you shut up?" Suppose God did that—either didn't permit praying at all or, if He did, ruled out our pleas for comfort? Imagine what we'd miss.

The benefits are enormous for husbands and wives who fall on their knees before God in times of stress and crisis. It can relieve their fears and kindle their hope, often holding them and their marriage together when they might otherwise fall apart.

Even praying about matters that are less than crises can relieve anxiety and stress. Making decisions, for example, can be quite upsetting, and it's something couples do daily. Surveys show that one area of decision-making, spending money, causes more arguments among married couples than anything else. Praying about economic and other questions can help couples consider God's will for their lives. It can give them courage and serenity, being assured they have committed themselves and their judgments to Him.

I am not suggesting, however, that we use prayer as a way to comfort ourselves over hasty or foolish decisions. Many of us have used in a wrong way Psalm 37:5 which promises: "Commit your way to the LORD; trust in him, and he will do this." We've baptized our unwise, selfish ventures in prayer thinking God is obliged to make them succeed. Prayer, however, is not like waving a magic wand or rubbing a rabbit's foot. What we say about the next benefit will point out why.

Prayer enables us to comply with the will of God

Prayer, if it is to be heard, must be according to His will (1 John 5:14-15). The postscript of every prayer should be: "Thy will be done" (Luke 22:42). Committing our way to God includes dedicating ourselves to His way. Prayer not only enables us to ask what we want but to question what God wants.

Prayer as a couple, then, becomes a joint quest for God's will. This will help you make decisions and will, in turn, make you more one-minded, more united in your dreams and objectives. Prayer may not make it easy for you to agree, but it should make it easier. And you will feel like you are a team, pulling together, playing the same game, as a husband stated: "Our paths become parallel instead of divergent or crossing each other." You will have what another couple has: "a sense of peace knowing we're heading through life toward the same direction."

There is yet another purpose for praying and it is contained in another type of prayer that we will discuss next.

TWO TALK

- What reasons to pray make the most sense to you?
- What reasons are there that you should pray together as a couple?

SYSTEMATICALLY INTERCEDE FOR OTHERS

Perhaps nothing contributes more to involving a couple with the outside world than praying for other people. In intercession, they establish a three-way connection: to God, each other, and to others. It fixes their attention on world events, sets their minds on other people's concerns, and extends their feelings beyond themselves.

Paul mentioned intercession in a list of four types of prayer: "I urge, then, first of all, that requests, prayers, intercession and thanksgiving be made for everyone" (1 Timothy 2:1). The Greek word for "requests" here would better be translated "appeals," depicting a note of urgency. It implies praying to God as you would plead to a king for favor or for a friend in trouble.

Though prayer, of course, should not be a substitute for helping others, it can still be a tremendous support to others. Frequently, people in crisis have been propped up by others praying for them, even drawing strength from just knowing they were.

Yet, praying for others is not just a show of support. God seems to respond in special ways to intercessory prayer. The Apostle Paul was fanatical about getting Christians to pray for each other. He constantly requested prayer for himself and his ministry: "Pray for me, that whenever I open my mouth words may be given me," he asked the Ephesians (6:19). He seemed to count on those prayers for his success: "I know that through your prayers, and the help given by the Spirit of Jesus Christ, that which has happened to me will turn out for my deliverance" (Philippians 1:19). Frequently, he mentioned praying for other Christians and he urged them to do so for each other: "Pray . . . with all kinds of prayers and requests . . . be alert and always keep on praying for all the saints" (Ephesians 6:18).

Though Christians may disagree about the practice of faith healing, they agree that God does sometimes heal, perhaps not always in some miraculous, out of the ordinary way. James tells sick people to call the elders of the church to pray over them . . ."and the prayer offered in faith will make the sick person well" (James 5:15). Whatever prayer's role in physical health, there can be no doubt about intercession's contribution to spiritual growth. Paul's descriptions of his prayers for others are rich treatises on spirituality. The following is only one of several:

I pray that out of his glorious riches, he may strengthen you with power, through his Spirit in your inner being, so that Christ may dwell in your hearts through faith. And I pray that you, being rooted and established in love, may have power, together with all the saints, to grasp how wide and long and high and deep is the love of Christ, and to know this love that surpasses knowledge—that you may be filled to the measure of all the fullness of God (Ephesians 3: 17-19).

Interceding for others is also a way to participate in someone else's ministry, something the Bible calls a "partnership in the gospel" (Philippians 1:3). A couple in Moline, Iowa can be partners with missionaries in the Ukraine, social workers in Honduras, a youth worker in Chicago's inner city, and on and on. We are dazzled that we can instantly connect with someone nearly anywhere in the world through E-mail. Yet, we've always been able to do it through prayer. Intercession provides couples with a satisfying mutual ministry with others.

Besides taking the time to pray for others, you may need to take some time to learn what to pray for. Praying informed prayers about the specific needs of others is a remarkable and unselfish act. You may want to think about how you can systematically intercede in this way.

You may do something quite simple: talk with each other about those you know who need prayer. Look into your heart to find who are you concerned about. Is it the kid you read about in the newspaper who lost his parents in an auto accident? Is it a person at work you haven't had time to mention to your husband? Talk awhile before you pray. What's happening in these people's lives, their agonies, dreams, or goals? What do you think God would have us pray for them? Such a discussion, by the way, is not only a help to others but also to your marriage, strengthening your intimacy and friendship by mutually sharing in each other's interests and network of acquaintances. Then, pray.

Of course, you can try to be more systematic: writing names in a notebook, or making a card file of missionaries, Christian leaders, and institutions. You might just use one manila folder to keep missionary letters in or save the list of requests in the church bulletin each week. The ministry will not necessarily stop with prayer, but, as it so often does, it leads them to be involved in other ways. Praying for some missionaries' financial needs often leads to giving to them; interceding for the poor farmers of Honduras opens our hands to help. This purpose, too, is behind praying together, since prayer can lead you to joint efforts to help others.

TWO TALK

- Share with each other when your prayers for someone have been answered.

- How could you improve your praying for others?

STOP AND LISTEN ONCE IN A WHILE

Prayer as a medium for receiving messages from God has become fashionable today. Popular books on the spiritual disciplines propose we should talk to God less and start listening more. Richard Foster, along with many Roman Catholic mystics, recommends a type of prayer called "centering prayer." This requires silence: both outward and inner. A person must get alone without distracting noises and then meditate quietly so that God can make Himself known to us once we open the door to the inner room of our souls. Foster claims God speaks to us in our dreams and recommends recording and analyzing them to decipher God's message.

Though Foster bases listening prayer on his Quaker tradition, he, like others, draws heavily on medieval mystics. Before practicing listening prayer, a Christian should decide whether God promises to speak to us today and, if so, how?

Foster, agreeing with the founder of the Quakers, believes

God will reveal Himself today just as He did in biblical times. God can give us clear directions today just as He did Ananias when He told him to go to a specific street named Straight (Acts 9:10-16).

Those who disagree with Foster readily concur God has spoken to people in the past: directly, as when Christ spoke and indirectly through visions and dreams. This speaking is what theologians call *revelation*. However, they contend that such clearcut revelation has come only at special times and is not promised for us today. Their reasoning is that God has already spoken and His message is written for us in Scripture (the recording of this message, theologians call *inspiration*). They follow the Protestant Reformers of the sixteenth century who came to this conclusion, particularly because of the trouble caused throughout church history by those who claim to have direct messages from God. Often, these messages contradicted the biblical message or were in conflict with other Christians who also claimed theirs came directly from God. Since Scripture already contains what we need to know from God, the Reformers contended, we don't need God to continue to speak miraculously and directly to us.

To explore this issue in depth and be fair to those on all sides, we would need a lot more space than we have; our briefly stated opinion will have to do. We believe that in a certain sense God speaks to us today but that we should be careful to define what that means. It's doubtful He speaks to us now as clearly as He did to Ananias, Jeremiah, or Abraham. To them and other biblical characters, the message was clearly from God, often authenticated by miracles or their fulfilled prophecies. We don't believe this kind of certainty is promised to us today.

However, because the Holy Spirit indwells those who trust in Christ, it is reasonable to believe that He can guide our thoughts and impress upon us certain ideas when we quietly meditate on some problem or a passage of Scripture. James, for example, encourages us to pray for wisdom. We shouldn't doubt that God can give us insight and direction. But, we should be careful not to equate that with God's speaking during the time He was giving a body of revelation to be deposited in Scripture.

If, however, in some less certain way God speaks to us today, our major difficulty is distinguishing His voice from our thoughts.

Foster claims the distinction can be made, but he doesn't explain how. "With time and experience you will be able to distinguish readily between mere human thought that may bubble up to the conscious mind and the True Spirit which inwardly moves upon the heart."[12]

We suggest any insight or inclination we get during meditation should be carefully judged in the light of Scripture and coupled with sound reasoning and gathering of facts. Being too sure we have heard from God may cause us to make serious mistakes in personal decisions or misdirect others by passing on to them a *word* from God which really isn't.

It seems there is no harm in suggesting we ask God to guide us while we quietly contemplate an issue in our lives or focus on a passage of Scripture. This type of meditation is taught in Scripture itself. The "blessed man" of the first Psalm delights in the law of the LORD and on it "he meditates day and night" (v. 2). Yet, this is different from the practice many teach today. Biblical meditation was like a cow chewing a cud, the mind taking some ideas and chewing on them. But the "centering of the mind," promoted by many today involves emptying the mind, not filling it, like being a cow without a cud. "Centering prayer presupposes that God makes His presence known from within . . . to quiet the mind those who pray repeat some 'sacred word,' like *God* or *Jesus* to center the mind. All other thoughts, even the most religious, are to be pushed aside until eventually—with practice, nothing remains but the presence of God."[13]

This is quite comparable to eastern forms of meditation that aim to lose one's sense of self and merge with the "Cosmic Mind."

Foster distances himself from this by suggesting that when Christians meditate they concentrate on some Scriptural verse or event, a personal problem, image, or emotion. Though he suggests we empty our minds, he means by that to avoid other distracting thoughts than those we want to "center" on.[14]

With the proper precautions and the right understanding, Christians can benefit from meditation. Though we don't know of many couples who practice it together, it is possible; we do it from time to time. After asking God to guide us, we close our eyes, and silently concentrate on something, a problem, a person or a statement of Scripture. After a short while, we share and discuss with each other what came to our minds.

This emphasis on meditation is catching on, no doubt, because modern people need it so badly. We are so continually drenched by noise and immersed in activity that we need to slow down and be quiet. By urging us to periodically meditate, Foster and others are doing us a favor.

TWO TALK

- Do you agree with the authors that God doesn't speak today as He did in biblical times?

- Do you think prayer should include listening to God?

PRAY CREATIVELY

Too often, praying together means this: You pray for awhile and then I'll pray for a while. Two things happen: You lose your concentration while the other is praying and you end up praying the same old prayers over and over again. The end result: dull and eventually done with. As one husband said, "The times were so dry and seemingly unproductive that they eventually just stopped."

Being more inventive will make your praying more interesting. To do so, you need to start with your goals. You need to know where you are going before you decide how to get there. If your goal is to get to the center of a lake, you don't choose a train to get you there. Method must match your aim.

So, ask yourself "What is the purpose of our praying together right now?" Are you going to worship, celebrate, confess, intercede, ask God for something, or simply talk to or listen to God? There is no need to do all of these in every session. Say, for example, we ask, "How shall we talk to God together tonight?"—no agenda, no special rituals to follow, no special high-sounding "spiritual" lingo required—just simply talk with God together. Perhaps one of you will open up and say, "God, we are grateful You'll hear us, and we don't have any agenda, but we'd like to share with You what's going on in our lives and some of our feelings and thoughts and I've been thinking about . . ." Then, the other can follow, based in part on thoughts provoked by the first one's prayers. Maybe, after the second one has prayed, the one who prayed first will pray again. And on and on you go. The technical name for this is "conversational prayer." Sometimes you can modify it a bit by making the rule that each time you pray you keep it brief. Or add another suggestion: that you are free to interrupt each other when one of you triggers a thought. "Yes, God, I was thinking about that too, and in my opinion, I would like to ask You about it to. . . ." Simple, isn't it? Yes, as easy as talking. In the process you may end up doing many types of prayer, worshiping God at one moment and interceding the next.

You can constantly modify your approach—to give another example: sentence prayers, used when your aim is to pray briefly about a lot of things. Decide you are both going to repeatedly finish the sentence: "Lord, something that I need or would like to see happen that I want to ask You about is . . ." "God, a sin or fault that I would like to confess is . . ."

Keep in mind, even when praying, you don't have to talk out loud. Simply discuss a problem, hold hands, and silently pray. This is especially good for those who aren't yet comfortable praying out loud before someone. Or you can write your prayer requests on paper, perhaps in a notebook. Some people use their computers to record their prayers.

Now, how about prayer as listening to God. Pick something out that's relevant to you: a personal problem, a question, a decision that needs to be made. Meditate on it for five minutes, then talk about it. Meditating on a Scripture verse this way can be extremely exciting and enriching. Perhaps, while you are each meditating, you could write out what you have been thinking; then you could read each other's report and discuss it.

It's not a bad idea to follow your feelings once in a while. Sometimes you will feel more like praising God than you will interceding for others and of course at times the reverse may be true. Before starting your devotion, ask each other: What should be the goal of our time together? Once that's clear, you may discover a unique and effective way to achieve it.

TWO TALK

- Do you like the idea of conversational prayer?
- Do you think it's helpful to use some creative ways of praying?

PRAY ANYTIME, ANYWHERE

When Paul asked us to pray without ceasing, he obviously didn't mean we could constantly be mouthing prayers to God or thinking of Him every second.

The phase he used, *without ceasing*, elsewhere in Greek literature describes a person with a hacking cough. It refers to something that is done periodically and frequently; so should our praying be. Thinking of prayer as something brief and relevant may open up scores of opportunities for you to pray together, even if you are very busy. Just slip in a few moments with God here and there: while riding in your car, during a lull in the evening (as rare as they might be), while lying in bed, etc.

Accept Gods's invitation to "approach the throne of grace with confidence, so that we may receive mercy and find grace to help in our time of need" (Hebrews 4:16). Belonging to a prayer chain can help you do this. These are systems designed for sharing urgent prayer requests quickly to large numbers of people, in which you are assigned to phone someone after receiving a call yourself. After receiving your call, simply turn off the television or stop whatever else you're doing and immediately pray about the request before you phone it to someone else.

Many couples in our survey said they prayed immediately when learning of people in trouble:

"When we hear a family member or close friend is experiencing a difficult time, we will often stop what we are doing and pray for the person."

"We could be driving on the highway, see an accident and pray for the health and safety of those involved."

"After a time of good communication—where one of us shares some deeper fear or concern—afterward we will pray and turn over to God what we've discussed."

TWO TALK

- When have you prayed spontaneously and informally?
- Do you think it's a good idea to try to pray together anytime and anywhere?

PRAY FOR EACH OTHER

There's a special bond between you when you hear your partner pray for you or hear him or her say, "I'll be praying for you."

Her marriage in trouble, an idea popped into Carol's mind: Pray for Larry. She resisted, but the marriage kept getting worse. Finally, she began praying for him and eventually asked Larry to pray with her.

Though they were Christians, they had no idea how to pray

and were hesitant and awkward. Carol suggested that at first each one write down on a piece of paper what they wanted his or her spouse to pray for him or her about. Then, they exchanged their lists and prayed. "Clumsily, we got through—each praying for the other's requests," she later wrote. "I was amazed at how touched I was to hear Larry praying for me. I couldn't remember the last time I'd heard some prayer just for my concerns." She continued to share how praying had renewed their relationship.

Pray for one another. The marriage you improve might be your own.

In this chapter, we haven't said everything about prayer—but, just about. Now, there's little left to do, but pray. But, first, perhaps you'd like to talk about it.

TWO TALK

Based on what you have read in this chapter and discussed together, summarize the ways you might improve your praying together.

TWO-GETHER
TIMES

- *Silent Prayer*

  This TWO-GETHER TIMES is for those who don't yet feel comfortable praying out loud together. This is a simple effective way to more toward that goal.

  1. Talk briefly about some person or situation that concern you both that you would like to pray about.

  2. Bow your heads (and hold hands, if you like) and each pray silently about your request.

3. Now talk about another request, pray silently. Continue to discuss and pray as long as you like.

- *Reading a Prayer*

  This TWO-GETHER TIMES is, like the one above, for those who yet don't feel comfortable praying out loud together. Reading a prayer is a nonthreatening way to start doing that. This one is taken from Scripture. Besides finding prayers there, you'll find them in the back of hymnals or in devotional books or in books of prayers. Also, remember, you can recite or read the Lord's Prayer recorded in Matthew 6:9-13.

  1. Each of you read Psalm 138 silently.

  2. Discuss what parts of the psalmist's prayer express ideas you would like to say to God.

  3. Read out loud together the Psalm as your prayer or else one of you read the first half and the other the second.

- *Reading a Prayer*

  Follow the same procedure as the previous TWO-GETHER TIMES using Psalm 143.

- *Writing a Prayer*

  1. Each of you look at all or some of the following verses to decide which you would like to rewrite in your own words as a prayer: Psalm 25:1-11;. Psalm 63:1-8.

  2. Each of you write your own prayer; discuss any questions or ideas that may come up as you do.

  3. Each of your read your prayer out loud.

- *Writing a Prayer*

  Follow the same procedure as the previous time together using Psalm 139:1-18.

- *Completion Sentence Prayers*

  This TWO-GETHER TIMES could be used repeatedly. It is intended to prompt you to petition God for various concerns.

  1. Begin with the first of these completion sentences. Each of you pray by finishing the sentence; you may pray more than once. Pray back and forth until you are ready to go to the next completion sentence.

  2. Move to the next completion sentence and pray as you did for the first, continue through the list, and pray about as many as you like.

  Completion sentences:

  1. Lord, today I am especially grateful for . . .

  2. God, one of the persons I am most concerned about is . . . and I pray for . . . that You will . . .

  3. Lord, I am concerned about a problem in our lives and I pray . . .

  4. Lord, one of the events in the news that concerns me is . . . and I pray that . . .

  5. God, for our pastor and his family I pray . . .

  6. For a missionary that we know . . . I pray . . .

  7. A situation or challenge in our church that is . . . I pray . . .

- *Conversation Prayer*

  This type of praying can be done often. Think of it as your socializing with God together.

  1. One of you begin by saying anything to God that comes to your mind; make your prayer brief; then stop to allow your partner to pray.

  2. The partner should pray briefly about anything, perhaps continuing the prayer that the other prayed.

  3. Continue in this way, following these guidelines.

     a. Feel free to interrupt your partner, adding to their prayer or agreeing with it.
     b. Allow the other person's prayer to stimulate your thinking about what you should pray for.
     c. Let your conversation with God wander.

- *Meditative Prayer*

  In this TWO-GETHER TIMES you'll practice listening to God.

  1. Choose a problem, or a subject that you would like to meditate about. Perhaps it's a decision you are currently wrestling with, a problem in the family, or some issue you have been thinking about.

  2. One of you ask God to guide you as you think about this.

  3. With eyes closed, focus your attention on the matter or verse you have selected. Try to do this for more than five minutes, which may seem like a long time. Your mind will wander at times, but stay with it, guiding your mind

to think about some part of the matter noting where you mind goes with it.

4. Now share with each other what you have been thinking.

5. Complete this TWO-GETHER TIMES by one or both of you praying.

- *Meditating on Scripture*

   Follow the instructions above using a verse of Scripture. Choose a verse or two from Psalm 23.

- *Praying About Goals and Dreams*

   1. Each of you share a dream you have for your own life or for your life together. Spend some time discussing these aspirations.

   2. Each of you pray about the other's dream asking God to fulfill it if it is His will.

- *Praying for Each Other*

   This is an example of using Scripture as a basis for praying. You did this in TWO-GETHER TIMES n previous chapters.

   1. Read out loud Colossians 2:9-12.

   2. Each of you then pray for the other using this prayer as a basis for your petition. You may use the same words as the Scripture or paraphrase them. For example: "God, I pray my wife will be filled with knowledge of Your will; one of the areas she is especially concerned about lately is . . . "etc. etc.

- *Interceding for Others*

  1. Each of you tell of one person you would like to pray for.

  2. Discuss together what you think that person most needs from God.

  3. Based on your discussion, each of you pray for the person you chose.

  4. If you like, record in your notebook the needs of that person and what you prayed for them.

- *Interceding for Others Using Scripture*

  1. Each of you choose someone whose spiritual development you are concerned about.

  2. Using Ephesians 1:15 as a basis for your prayer, each of you pray for the person you chose. You may use the actual words of the Scripture or paraphrase them, even going beyond the Scripture as you are stimulated to do so.

- *Petitioning and Believing*

  1. Make a list of specific prayer requests that you would like to see answered within the next month or two.

  2. Pray these petitions to God.

  3. In the days and weeks to come try to remind each other to trust God to respond to these requests.

- *Confession*

  1. Read Psalm 51 out loud.

  2. Discuss what verses might be appropriate to you con

cerning some sin in your life. Briefly share these failures with each other.

3. Using the Scripture you have chosen, each of you confess your sin and thank God for His forgiveness.

- *Give a Blessing (Short Version)*

This can be a very brief exercise or it could be extended into a longer one. Some couples make a regular practice of doing this once a week, perhaps at Friday's meal time. If you have children, they can be included. It's a great way to affirm and express your concern for each other.

The short version is simply as follows: Each of you, looking at the other (holding hands, if you like), says out loud: "(Name), I bless you today for . . . " Or you may say "(Name), I pray for you today that . . . " Here's an example: "Chick, today I pray for you that you will make it through the present busy schedule. I sense the pressure you are feeling, and I wish for you that it may soon be relieved but, in the meantime, that you will have strength to handle it."

- *Giving a Blessing (Longer Version)*

1. Each of you share with the other what you believe are the matters that are of most concern to the other. Then, each of you respond to what the other has said, correcting what he or she has said, or explaining your concern for these matters; you may even add to what was said.

2. After your discussion, each of you give a blessing to each other following the instructions of the previous TWO-GETHER TIMES.

CHAPTER FIVE

Studying Two-gether

Store up my commands within you,
turning your ear to wisdom and applying your
heart to understanding.
—Proverbs 2:1-2

E ven though appropriate, we hesitated calling this chapter "Studying Two-gether" because the word *studying* can conjure up gloomy images for many people: painfully stuffing facts into our skulls in order to put them on an exam paper, abandoned and forgotten; pouring over boring glossy pages of texts; held captive in *study* halls, fidgeting restlessly while waiting for a bell to liberate us. For some, that kind of studying is as exciting as summer school homework. Even the Bible warns: "Of making many books there is no end, and much study wearies the body" (Ecclesiastes 12:12).

Yet, studying involves much more than thick books and extends far beyond stuffy classrooms. If we define it properly, hardly a moment goes by without it. "To acquire knowledge" is one definition and we are constantly doing that in many ways. Perhaps, you were just *studying* Greg Norman's golf swing on TV in order to fine-tune your own. Or, to determine whether you might invite your partner to bed with you, you were *studying* his or her face. You might have just clicked off the Internet where you were surfing for how to treat the disease on your rose plants.

Studying involves more than picking up facts and ideas like

flowers from a field. It involves pondering those ideas, evaluating, and relating them to what we already know and sort of forming them into a bouquet of truth to inspire and guide us. Studying isn't just acquiring, it's thinking, which some critics of modern culture say is in short supply. With complicated technology we disseminate and gather data with amazing efficiency, but we lack expertise in using it, they claim. Figuring out what to do with information is what study is all about. Study makes the difference between harboring ideas in your head, which is knowledge, and discerning how to put them to use, which is wisdom. Study is something we do daily, like wondering how a new job will play or what to fix for supper. Study isn't just for scholars and scientists.

Living requires it. Unlike animals that survive by instinct, we must continually form new ways to cope with the problems and challenges. Studying is looking ahead with our minds. It is what a scouting party is to a group of combat soldiers, what diagnosis is for a physician, what a test drive is to a mechanic. By it, we analyze, spy out the situation so that we may successfully act. We cannot effectively move ahead without looking ahead.

And it's an active process, not a passive one, *studying* a television program and not just *watching* one. Study isn't just soaking up knowledge; it's reaching out and taking it.

This is why study is so essential for spiritual growth. Too often, our spiritual learning is passive, listening to a radio program or a sermon. We receive ideas, but we don't react to them. Because we haven't really thought much about them, they drop from our minds like darts that haven't stuck to the dart board. Yet, to engage life as a Christian we must engage our minds. The spiritual life is a mental pursuit. It is not just a quest to receive truth, but to understand, remember, and experience it. "Sanctify them by the truth; your word is truth," Jesus prayed for His followers. "The truth will set you free," he said. Liberty springs from truth and truth from study, which is often an arduous, painstaking task.

Growing Christians must practice mental aerobics. We must love God with our minds as well as our hearts and souls.

Scripture insists the need to learn is urgent. We are told to search for wisdom "as for hidden treasure" (Proverbs 2:4); it's that valuable. We thought of this when we viewed the gold bars, silver vases, and sparkling jewelry found by the famous treasure hunter Mel Fisher. Only part of the cache of the sunken Spanish galleon *Nuestra Señora del Atocha* was on display in our area, but we marveled at what we saw. The overall find, worth billions, included quarts of emeralds and bars of silver stacked like cordwood.

Yet, finding these treasures took Fisher more than fifteen years and required a costly search of seventy million dollars.

Wisdom, too, only comes to those who "look for it as if for silver" (Proverbs 2:4). Study demands long hours and hard work. Champions of the spiritual disciplines claim there can be no real spirituality without it. While celebration, worship, and prayer supply much of the motivation to grow, study provides the direction. Study shapes and tints our thoughts. It strengthens our thinking like lifting weights builds muscles; it enlarges and stretches our minds and expands our souls. It enables us to relate successfully to others and make our lives count. Christians cannot live by emotion alone. Getting high on Jesus, Richard Foster warns, is no substitute for knowing about Him. "Many are hampered and confused in the spiritual walk by simple ignorance of the truth."[1] We must study, he insists. Dallas Willard is emphatic: "We must devote long hours to it."

Studying is probably best done alone. Instructors on the spiritual disciplines almost always link it with the discipline of solitude. Alone and quiet, we can concentrate better. You can read silently by yourself much faster than you can out loud with your partner. Pursuing answers to burning questions and rambling through Scripture and other books is far easier by yourself than with someone else.

- Are you motivated to search for wisdom?
- How do you do it?
- Do you agree that studying alone is easier than studying with someone?

DETERMINE WHAT TO EXPECT

Yet, doing some studying together makes sense. But because it is so different from doing it alone, you'll need to decide exactly what you intend to get out of it. If you expect to cover a lot of ground or get a lot of new information, you may be disappointed. One-on-one studying is rather awkward, since most of us have done so little of it, apart from being tutored or taking music lessons. In school or church, we primarily learn with a large or small group of people, so we're well acquainted with methods used there. However, these methods aren't effective in one-on-one study, and we're often not acquainted with those that are. Some couples who try, eventually give up. One man conceded, "Primarily we pray together. We have only once tried to read a book together." Another lamented: "For a time, we tried reading together Oswald Chamber's *My Utmost for His Highest*. The times were so dry, seemingly unproductive, that they eventually just stopped."

Because of this we think it's best to be realistic about what to expect from studying together. Couples reported to us the following.

Learning from each other

For one thing, you can learn from each other. Reported one couple: "We sometimes discuss an issue that springs from a question asked of my wife at her work (her coworkers know that her husband is a seminarian, so she is seen as a *de facto* Bible expert and theologian by marriage)."

"We help each other with spiritual questions and struggles," said another couple. They also help each other make judgments about issues and evaluate new ideas they are exposed to. Since many political, moral, and spiritual issues are tough to solve, husbands and wives can profit from each other's insights. A husband explains: "My wife has a low view of her own faith and spirituality, but I have seen again and again that it is her and not me whom God is using to communicate meaningfully to our family. Whereas I may be able to quote Scripture and scholars, she often more clearly sees the issue at stake and has accompanying spiritual insight into the questions."

Being intellectually intimate

Studying together produces an important form of intimacy: intellectual intimacy. Many couples report that in their marriage there is too little meeting of the minds. What could be more profound and mentally stimulating than studying spiritual matters together? Nearly nothing, said one husband: "While neither of us is, by nature, a very open person, talking about spiritual issues gives us a great sense of intimacy." However it's done, study can create some *quality time*, which most couples long for.

Keeping up with each other

Marriages, like clothes, are likely to come apart at the seams, and one of the most vulnerable seams is a couple's worldview: their values, morals, and spiritual outlook. Often, when they marry, their worldviews are similar. But, when their experiences and their thinking take them in different directions, they grow apart. This particularly happens when one person's spiritual progress rapidly out-paces the other's. In the seminary setting, this often occurs with one spouse studying Bible and theology full-time, the other working to support them financially. Their spiritual growth is as uneven as one fertilized plant growing beside one that is not. Studying together can help prevent that from happening.

It is in our minds that our view of the world is lodged. Fighting off a secular view of life is a mental battle. "Do not conform any longer to the pattern of this world, but be transformed by the renewing of your mind" (Romans 12:2). Daily, by contact with the media and others, we are bombarded by secular views, practices, and attitudes—"the pattern of this world." Our minds and feelings are constantly polluted by the outlook on life that says, "There is no God," which so easily soaks into our pores and eventually our souls. This needs to be washed away. Our minds need constant renewal. That occurs when we open the Scriptures or open ourselves to other Christians, which instantly plunges us into a different worldview.

Studying spiritual truths together, we are more likely to maintain a similar outlook that will prevent us from being pulled in different directions by two different streams. Couples expressed this experience in different ways: "Our mutual understanding and appreciation of the other's view of ultimate things helps communication tremendously, as it informs our understanding of basic worldviews." "We share the same value system; we know where each other is coming from."

Christians should share a sort of one-mindedness. Said Paul: "Be of one mind, live in peace" (2 Corinthians 13:11). Apparently, he wasn't asking us to always think alike but to retain a spirit of cooperation and unity. Yet, he sometimes suggests that keeping your thinking in sync will help keep your relationship intact: "That you agree with one another so that there may be no divisions among you and that you may be perfectly united in mind and thought" (1 Corinthians 1:10). One couple expressed graphically what sharing their faith does for their relationship: "We have a sense of peace knowing we're heading through life toward the same direction."

Stimulating each other's thoughts

Some couples put a lot of emphasis on study's helping them understand each other by grasping each other's point of view.

They try to discuss things. "We read a couples' devotional book with Scripture, then discuss it. We alternate reading [i.e., one time the husband, next time the wife] and read out loud." Some report just reading and discussing Scripture. Sometimes, they simply talk about what they've been learning separately. "We share and discuss what we have been learning in our separate quiet times and what we have been reading in books."

Blessed are those who interact. Couples should do in their homes what's practiced in good classrooms: deliberating, disputing, and debating issues. To do this, you must permit each other to state opinions, encouraging each to think for him or herself.

Granted, it's not always pleasant. Sparks sometimes fly when we knock heads together. But the little spark can create light, especially if you allow each other to disagree without criticism.

This is especially true when the heads belong to very dissimilar people, who are often found married to each other. By interacting, we challenge each other from different perspectives, a male or female view, for example. Couples have a priceless opportunity to mentally and spiritually stretch each other, to broaden and deepen their grasp of life and spiritual matters—if they will be open to pondering each other's insights. They lose a great deal if one has information or understanding that could help the other but for various reasons is thwarted from sharing it, either because we are too busy, too proud to listen, or too fearful of hurting each other.

Giving God a chance to speak to you together

As we've noted, we can't be confident that the thoughts we have when we are praying or meditating are the voice of God. But, we can be certain of it when we are studying Scripture. Christians generally agree that God speaks through His written Word.

Christian couples who study that Word open themselves up to a timely message from God. Of course, that message can get through to them when they individually study. But, when God's message hits home to both of them they may be more attentive, particularly when that message applies to their joint life such as when in their decisions about financial matters they need direction or, in their distress over a snag in their relationship, they need encouragement. Also, when studying together, they have a chance to relay to each other messages they are perceiving. As one husband reported, "My wife, more so than I, will sometimes express a feeling or specific leading from God."

Obviously, whenever couples jointly receive a message from God and act on it, they can produce crucial turning points in their lives. Life, then, becomes a venture with God. He leads; they follow, as one husband wrote: "One thing that we have found to be true is the amazing faithfulness of God in guiding us, or giving us direction for our future. He has always provided us both with confidence and a certain amount of clarity when it comes to His will for our life together."

TWO TALK

Discuss:

- Considering the purposes just mentioned in this chapter, which mean the most to us?

- Is there a chance we can accomplish any of them?

EFFECTIVELY STUDY THE BIBLE

Sounds awesome: God is going to speak to us through Scripture. So you open it and read. Puzzled, your face showing it, you ask, "What did He say?" The answer: "I'm not sure." Face it, God's message is not always obvious. The Bible is an old book, some sections with a very ancient look, more like a cryptogram than a telegram. Scholars analyze and probe obscure passages, debating endlessly which of five or six possible meanings is correct.

Yet, it is possible to understand accurately the Bible. And every part of it has a message from God. "All Scripture is useful," said Paul. To find that message we merely have to follow some guidelines when we study it.

Look for the author's meaning

First, you have to try to find out what the author of the passage meant when he wrote it. People go wrong when they ask, "What does this mean to me?" before asking, "What did it mean when it was written?" Take, for example, what Jeremiah said to the nation of Israel: "In vain shalt thou use many medicines; for thou shalt-not be cured" (Jeremiah 46:11, KJV). Taken alone, we might think God is telling us to refuse any medical treatment.

Bill and Linda Barnhart thought so. Instead of calling a doctor for their sick two-year-old son Justin, they prayed. For months they watched Jason's stomach swell until eventually a tumor, they later learned, had engulfed the left kidney, almost totally constricting the digestive system and sapping most of his nutrition. Jason starved to death. Because doctors believed medical care might have saved him, Bill and Linda Barnhart were prosecuted for not seeking that care. Authorities in Pennsylvania concluded that the Barnharts had a right to their religious beliefs but not the right to impose them on their son.

When reporters asked them where they got those beliefs, Bob, Bill's brother, quoted Jeremiah 46:11 and said, "I want you to read that and see what you expect somebody to take out of that. I'd like you to tell me what your interpretation is. I want you to study the whole thing out."

"We feel that God wrote this Bible," Bob said. "Now how are you gonna walk up to the pearly gates when the time comes and say, 'God, you didn't mean Jeremiah 46:11.' If he didn't mean it, why did he put it in the Bible?"[2]

The Barnharts' tragic dilemma shows how important it is to be sure to interpret Scripture correctly. Too often we just spot an idea, take it at face value, and apply it without regard for its primary meaning, the one intended by the author.

Even Jesus' disciples made this mistake. Jesus told them, "Watch out for the yeast of the Pharisees and that of Herod" (Mark 8:15). Apparently, not grasping what He really meant, they naively responded by discussing with one another, saying, "It is because we have no bread" (Mark 8:16). They heard "yeast" and thought "bread"—that Jesus was worried about not having any—quite absurd since He had just miraculously produced enough to feed thousands of people. They missed the point big time, since by using the word "yeast," Jesus wasn't talking about bread but about unbelief. He was telling them to avoid the Pharisee's trait of failing to believe Jesus was the Son of God.

Some additional guidelines for studying the Bible will help us avoid this kind of misunderstanding.

Interpret the words and phrases in their context

Nobody interprets the meaning of words without the circumstances in which they were said. The comment, "He lifted his trunk," means something entirely different if the speaker is standing in front of an elephant at the zoo or in front of a luggage porter at the airport. The disciples would have understood Jesus if they had considered two things. First, they should have noticed that Jesus didn't just say "yeast," but "the yeast of Pharisees and that of Herod." Secondly, they should have thought about the context of His statement. At the time, these men were fiercely opposing Jesus. Seeing that Jesus was cautioning them about something that pertained to His enemies, they could have figured out what He was saying.

The key to understanding Jeremiah's statement also lies in looking carefully what's written before and after it. Out of context, the phrase "In vain shalt thou use many medicines," could be used as an attack against physicians and their cures. However, Jeremiah didn't have all doctors in mind; just those in ancient Egypt. He simply meant that Egypt was to be punished by God and no remedies would help alleviate the suffering.

To find what this passage says to us, we must first discover what it meant to those to whom it was written. After all, the passage did not first address us.

Adam and Eve, for example, were told not to eat of the tree in the middle of the garden. They would die if they did (Genesis 2:17). Obviously, this passage does not mean that anyone with a tree in the middle of their garden should not pick its fruit. This warning was given to particular people at a particular time at a particular place.

This is true of much Scripture, probably the majority of it, since passages written directly for Christians of all times are in the minority. Even many of the teachings of Jesus were directed at people in His day and not us. Selling all possessions and giving the proceeds to the poor is not a requirement for all Christians even though Jesus did demand that one man do it.

Determine the type of literature

Next we must identify the literary form of the message since all types of literature are not interpreted the same way. This is even the case when we open our daily newspaper. You read an advertisement for a cure for baldness differently than you do a front-page news story. Editorials, comics, political cartoons, and other genres convey their message in different ways. So do the literary types in the Bible. The parables of Jesus are not to be read the same way as His sermons. Parable stories convey a truth, but the stories themselves may not be true; we don't expect them to be, and therefore, we don't interpret them as history.

The Bible contains poetry, historical narrative, prophesies, proverbs, poetry, and other literary forms. We must be careful not to read every passage as if it were a magazine's news report or a cookbook recipe. Some books of the Bible are like that. The letters of Paul, for example, are straightforward instructions and teaching. But, not every page of Scripture should be read in the same way. To do so can be misleading. Poetic phrases (and about one third of the Bible is poetry) are not to be taken as absolute statements of truth, without exception. In Psalm 91, the poet says "If you make the Most High your dwelling . . . then no harm will befall you, no disaster will come near your tent" (vv. 9, 10). Celebrating God's protection, the poet conveys the feeling of confidence of those who trust in Him. And we should think about and feel that assurance. But the phrase is not meant to be an absolute promise, for we know God does sometimes allow harm to come to those who rely on Him. In the Bible, many godly people suffered and, like Stephen, were murdered. Taken as a statement of fact, this verse would be wrong. Understood as poetry, it is not. Recognizing this does not discredit Psalm 91; it explains it.

Proverbs, too, is another form of literature that can be easily misunderstood. When written, Proverbs were taken to be moral lessons in a special package. They often convey their message by comparing concrete things with abstract ones, like our phrase "A rolling stone gathers no moss." Anyone (except a child, perhaps) who hears this doesn't think the speaker is talking about clean stones. Rather, we get the point: In life, don't stand still, keep moving.

Proverbs should not be interpreted like the statements "It's raining out" or "God so loved the world." We must see the principle they contain and not turn them into ironclad absolutes. The Hebrews tended to make general statements without worrying about exceptions to them, appealing to the reader's common sense to see this. For example, one Proverb states: "When a man's ways are pleasing to the Lord, he makes even his enemies live at peace with him" (16:7). Thus it is generally true that being rightly related to God will help you stay rightly related to others. But, this is not a promise meant to be without exception. Jesus, for example, obeyed God, yet His enemies murdered Him. Thinking God guarantees obedient Christians good personal relations will only disappoint you, just as turning Proverbs 22:6 into a promise disappoints many parents. "Training a child in the way he should go, and when he is old he will not turn from it" is not telling us parental training is always effective. It is simply confirming it is powerful. Some children are too foolish to follow their parents training; this, too is a major theme of the Proverbs. And in the Old Testament, it was the rebellious kids who were blamed, not the parents. Proverbial and poetic expressions not only teach us, they inspire us; they stir our emotions and arouse our faith.

Apparently, this is the reason the Bible contains so many different types of literature; each has its special purpose. Proverbs and parables make us think; they build conviction. Poetry strikes the many emotional strings of our soul. History provides examples for us to follow or avoid. Prophecy, which is often poetic, gives us stunning warnings of God's judgment along with exquisite pledges of His faithfulness. Recognizing this will permit us to respond to the powerful impact of each literary form.

We don't have to be literary scholars to do this. We simply have to avoid taking every verse of Scripture as if it were part of a legal document and note how it may express ideas in a different way. Reading one of a number of brief paperback books on the Bible's literature can also help such as *How to Read the Bible for All It's Worth* by Gordon D. Fee and Douglas Stuart, published by Zondervan Publishing House, 1982.

Watch for figures of speech

Metaphors, similes, and other figures of speech can be misleading, and the Bible is full of them. Not that the Bible can't be taken literally like books we normally read, but literally means *normally*. And normally, authors use a lot of figures of speech when writing. Poetry is saturated with figures of speech and is written in such a way as to appeal to the emotions. "The LORD tears down the proud man's house, but he keeps the widow's boundaries intact" is a way of telling us how God resists the proud and defends the helpless. But, obviously, all proud persons' roofs do not cave in on them. Jesus' use of similes and metaphors are usually not hard to understand: When He calls Himself the light of the world or a door, we get the point. Sometimes, His figures of speech can be confusing. For example, He recommends cutting off your hand if it causes you to sin. A famous Christian of the early church actually castrated himself because of this statement. Yet, Jesus was using a common form of expression in His day: exaggeration; He didn't intend His words to be taken at face value. He used Jewish hyperbole often. If you had faith the size of a mustard seed, He said, you could say to a mountain "Move from here to there" and "it will move" (Matthew 17:21). Besides the fact that no one, including Jesus, ever did this, it's obvious Jesus is exaggerating two things to show the power of faith: the faith as a tiny mustard seed and the task, the size of a mountain.

The Barnharts might have taken their dangerously ill son to a doctor had they had seen that Jeremiah was speaking figuratively. The poetic reference to medicine in Jeremiah's poetic passage is obviously a figure of speech. Since the prophet is referring to the wound to the whole nation, not its individuals, he is not referring to literal physical illnesses medicine. Rather, it's a forceful way to warn them that national attempts to save themselves from military attack were useless because God had ordered it.

Now, if these guidelines are new to you, you may be thinking Bible study to be too complicated to even try it. Not true. Most of the Bible is as easy to understand as your morning newspaper. Because we can't grasp it all doesn't mean we can't understand it at all. "I read the Bible like I eat chicken," an elderly pastor once told us. "I feast on what I can understand and when I come to the parts I can't, I lay them aside like bones."

We suggest, when you study as a couple, you focus on the obvious. Let the type of literature grip you as it was meant to. Don't quibble over every difficult figure of speech or the meaning of every phrase. For example, take the phrase in Psalm 23:

"You prepare a table before me in the presence of my enemies." The picture that most likely comes to mind is probably wrong: a table loaded with our favorite dishes and drinks while in the shadows all our grisly foes are looking on, paralyzed by God. Rather, the table is no doubt a piece of land, a high place, flush with grass for God's sheep to graze, securely protected from wolves and the like. Now does it really matter which is the correct picture? In one sense, yes, since we need to interpret accurately. But in this case it may not be so crucial, since the meaning comes through either way. A table prepared in the presence of enemies, however pictured in your mind, conveys the impact of the passage: God graciously provides for us while protecting us. In this case, the feeling—the stimulation to faith—is what counts. That's what the two of you should be looking for.

Then, lay aside the bones for in-depth personal study. At the end of the chapter we'll suggest some excellent tools for that. At times, together you might want to look for answers to tough questions in a Bible commentary or a dictionary, for example. But, in general, study together for other reasons—the ones we've already mentioned. Don't let the difficult and troublesome passages interfere with getting God's message to you.

Use other Scripture to interpret Scripture

To insure your getting the right interpretation, there is one more important guideline: let other parts of the Bible shed light on the passage you're studying. Sometimes passages are obscure, hard to figure out; but, in another place in the Bible, there are clear-cut statements on the same subject. It makes sense to accept the meaning of the easy-to-understand passage. When we study the Bible, we should constantly be comparing Scripture with other Scripture.

Thus, for example, it seems clear that we are saved by grace and not by works. The Apostle Paul states that clearly in several places. And other passages of Scripture point to the same truth. Yet, James seems to say the opposite.

Truth is determined not merely by individual passages but by the sum total of teaching on a subject. Therefore, any passage that seems to suggest that good works saves us should be interpreted in the light of the clearer message that they do not. Cults and others who deviate from Christianity often build their teaching on an obscure passage despite the fact that it is out of line with the whole. An incidental reference of Paul about people being baptized for the dead is taken by the Mormon church to teach that non-Christian dead people can be saved by some living Christian being baptized for them (1 Corinthians 15:29). Because this idea opposes everything other Scripture teaches us about personal responsibility and salvation we should avoid believing 1 Corinthians teaches it. We should interpret 1 Corinthians in the light of the whole instead of the reverse. Simply, Paul was referring to people who practice it, even though he himself did not believe it.

TWO TALK

- Which of the stated guidelines for studying Scripture are somewhat new to you?
- Are there any that are difficult to understand?
- Has the discussion of these guidelines been helpful?
- How and why?

USE SOME CREATIVE METHODS FOR READING AND STUDY

As is the case with the other disciplines, studying together loses its gusto if always done the same way. Couples confirm this. They tire of simply reading a page of a devotional book or the Bible and then praying. Creativity is not an end in itself. We are not trying to be innovative to be new. Nor is it to turn spiritual disciplines into fun and games. Rather, creativity enables us to do what we do with purpose. It suggests different ways to achieve the same goal: to enrich us spiritually so that we may worship and serve our Lord together. In all of life, we must use different means for different ends. We don't use a car to cross a lake or teach two-year-olds by lecturing to them for fifty minutes. The same is true for study.

Lethargy sets in when we use a method that is ineffective. You need to use methods that go beyond your acquiring knowledge to those that will make you interact with each other—to evaluate ideas, understand them, and put them to use. Your goal in studying with each other is to talk with each other and there are many ingenious ways to do that. Sometimes it's as simple as reading a passage, then discussing it.

"Our time together is often for discussion. We sometimes discuss a book or passage of Scripture that we have read and that seems particularly relevant," wrote one couple. Yet, most of us need a little more prodding to get us to open up to each other. Why not try reading a passage, then talking about what you do or don't understand? Then, briefly consult a Bible commentary for an answer to one of the questions. This will not only help you to interpret the passage carefully, it will give you something to talk about. You might skip reading a passage of Scripture for some of your sessions and read right out of a Bible commentary, devotional book, or even a book on a Christian view of marriage, discipleship, etc. Use the discussion questions that are sometimes included in these books. We have found the *Serendipity Bible* a wonderful tool for our Bible study.

Discussion can also be generated by your simply talking, without the Bible or any book in hand. One couple said, "We sometimes discuss an issue that springs from a question of my wife at her work." More than one couple reported reflecting together each week on the Sunday sermon or about what they've been learning in their personal "quiet time." It's powerful to probe each other with personal questions: "How do you feel about what the Psalmist said?" or "Did you ever have the same experience as the person in this passage?"

Briefly listening to an audio tape or watching a video can also provide a bit of variety in your approach. In our TWO-GETHER TIMES we will suggest lots of creative ways to get you started in experimenting with novel approaches to study.

TWO TALK

- List what creative ways you have used to study together.

- What other ways might you find effective?

PLAN YOUR TIME TOGETHER

Among the major reasons for not having devotionals together, couples list "not knowing what to do" and "lack of planning." To have effective TWO-GETHER TIMES you need to plan for them. A woman named Peggy once told us how it saves time.

> If you know what you are going to do, you can get right to it. Like if you are reading through the Gospel of John, you can turn your marker in your Bible and start. If you haven't decided beforehand, you waste a lot of time thinking about what to do. Sometimes, when that happens for our devotions at night before going to sleep, my husband will be fumbling through his Bible to find something to read while I lie beside him. By the time he finds something, I will have fallen asleep.

Planning doesn't have to be elaborate; it's just a matter of deciding what you are going to be doing for a certain period of time, perhaps study a book of the Bible or read together a devotional book or one on marriage. Few couples reported that they studied for very long periods of time, though one couple completed a rather ambitious study project. "We worked through a copy of Henry Blackaby's *Experiencing God* (five inductive studies each week, plus video) and sharing; it took us a year."

To have some variety and creativity some couples do different things on different days. For example, Monday: discuss and apply Sunday's sermon; Wednesday: read from Scripture and worship; Friday, intercede for missionaries and others. The TWO-GETHER TIMES suggestions of this book could be done in this way, taking one from the worship chapter one day, the celebration chapter the next, etc.

At the end of this book you'll find a list of resources to use when making your plans.

TWO TALK

- Which suggested plans mentioned did you like the most?

- Which would be more workable for you?

- What plan should you now make and try for a period of time?

STUDY INFORMALLY AND SPONTANEOUSLY

Discussing, reflecting, evaluating, and debating ideas can happen anytime and can easily be built into your life and relationship, especially if you deliberately choose to do so.

"Upon first seeing each other at the end of the day we discuss certain relevant spiritual thoughts or ideas we have cultivated." One couple reported regular interaction about spiritual matters: "We discussed spiritual issues in depth before we even got married, so we began our marriage very like-minded on a wide variety of spiritual topics. We also benefited from this early communication in that we felt comfortable discussing spirituality from day one."

Do this intentionally. Watch for opportunities: while riding in the car or lying in bed at night. Plan to share new ideas you have encountered or are wrestling with. Interact anytime. Get into each other's skulls and feelings. A Proverb says: "As iron sharpens iron, so one man sharpens another" (Proverbs 27:17). Make that happen in your relationship.

TWO TALK

- What opportunities for to study and interact together spontanenously and informally do we have that we might be overlooking?

- How could we capitalize on these times?

RELATE GOD'S TRUTH TO LIFE

Making truth relevant will put the most zest into your study. No matter what part of the Bible you study, there's a message there. Though reading the Bible sometimes resembles browsing in an antique shop with items you don't recognize or see any use for, you'll find priceless wisdom.

Whether in the New Testament or the Old, whether it's the prophets or the poets, whether its history or biography, there's something practical. "All Scripture is profitable," said Paul. Every page has ancient truth for modern times. A Filipino man tragically discovered how old crusty things can still have impact. He dug up a bomb that was dropped in World War Two and had laid buried for more than twenty-five years. In order to pry it apart and salvage its metal, he hammered and poked it. He died in the explosion.

God's word is like a weapon; it is quick and powerful, like a two edged sword. But, it's designed to develop, not destroy, us. And we study it not just to have full minds, but full lives. Making our faith determine how we live is a major discipline in itself. This is why we have devoted the following chapter to it, which we call "Growing Two-gether."

TWO-GETHER
TIMES

Keep in mind that these TWO-GETHER TIMES are to teach you how to study together. Therefore, their major goal is the acquisition and discussion of knowledge. The application of truth will be dealt with in the next chapter. However, you might want to bring into these TWO-GETHER TIMES practice of any of the other disciplines. You may end up discussing how a truth applies to life, or you may end by worshiping or celebrating or praying.

* *Observing and Interpreting a Passage of Scripture*

  One of the keys to having a good discussion of a passage of Scripture is the selecting of a passage that has a theme to it. You can usually do this by selecting a paragraph, which in many translations has a title at the beginning of it. Each of the following sections has a theme. By the questions we ask, we will try to help you identify it.

  1. Without reading the passage out loud, while each of you are looking at it, together make a list of what you observe in Colossians 1:1-8. Start with verse one and continue. To do this, tell each other only what you see; do not try to interpret. You may write them down if you like. For example, in verse one you see: "Paul calls himself an apostle. He refers to Jesus as Christ Jesus, not Jesus Christ. He says he is an apostle by God's will. He includes Timothy in the greeting and he calls him our brother."

  Continue through all eight verses. Try not to stop and discuss at length any one item until you have made your list.

2. Discuss together what has seemed most significant to you from all of these verses.

3. Share with each other any questions you have about the meaning of any of the words or statements. For example, "What is the meaning of 'bearing fruit?' in verse 6?"

4. Share with each other what you think these statements that you noted mean. Try to determine their meaning from the context and from what you know from other Scripture.

5. Especially note the various terms Paul uses to describe the Gospel and what he says about it.

6. From what is said about the Gospel here, discuss what you think the Gospel meant to Paul.

7. Discuss whether or not you agree with or fully understand what Paul says about the Gospel.

• *Observation and Interpretation of a Passage*

1. As in the previous TWO-GETHER TIMES, without reading the passage out loud, make a list of all that you see in Colossians 1:9-14.

2. Discuss what strikes you as new or significant.

3. Discuss what you have questions about or may not understand.

4. Share with each other possible answers to these questions or the meaning of items you've noted.

5. Especially discuss what Paul's view of a maturing Christian is from these verses.

6. Pray about what you have discussed.

- *Observtion and Interpretation of a Passage*

  1. As in the previous TWO-GETHER TIMES, without reading the passage out loud, make a list of all you see in Colossians 1:15-20.

  2. Especially note all that the passage says about Jesus.

  3. Discuss what is significant to you or what you may not understand.

  4. Share together any possible answers to your questions about meaning.

  5. Discuss how this passage makes you feel about God's Son.

  6. Pray together about what you have discussed.

- *Observation and Interpretation of a Passage*

  1. As in the previous TWO-GETHER TIMES, without reading the passage out loud, make a list of all you see in Colossians 1:21-27.

  2. Discuss what is significant to you or what you may not understand.

  3. Discuss whom you most identify with in this passage: the Colossians and the Gentiles or Paul. Discuss why.

  4. Share what you have to be thankful for from the truth of this passage.

  5. Pray about what you have discussed.

- *Observation and Interpretation of a Passage*

  1. As in the previous TWO-GETHER TIMES, without reading

the passage out loud, make a list of all you see in Colossians 1:28—2:5. Especially try to note everything that Paul says about his ministry.

2. Discuss what is significant to you or what you may not understand.

3. What does this passage tell you about what it is like to serve Christ?

4. Discuss if you identify with any of the things Paul says about his ministry or if you know anyone who may be like Paul in these struggles (your pastor, for example).

5. Pray about what you have discussed.

- *Using a Commentary to Study a Passage*

  Sometimes you can have a profitable study time by reading from a commentary on the book of the Bible you are studying. It's best to take just a short passage of Scripture, study it first, raising questions you might have, then consult the commentary for answers. Most Christian bookstores will have a number of commentaries on any book of the Bible. Some are based on the original language and are more difficult. Others are much easier to study. Be sure to get one that explains the details of the text. Here's how to use a commentary.

  1. Read out loud Colossians 2:6-15.

  2. Make all the observations you can about what is said here.

  3. List the questions you have about the meaning of terms and statements in this passage.

  4. Read a commentary to find answers to any questions you

have. You may choose to purchase to consult for further study of Colossians and to go back and answer questions you raised and couldn't answer in the above TWO-GETHER TIMES" passages.

- *Observing and Interpreting a Passage of Scripture*

  1. Read out loud Colossians 2:16-23.

  2. Note especially that there are three things the Colossians are to avoid, based on the following three statements: "Do not let anyone judge you" (verse 16); "Do not let anyone . . . disqualify you for the prize" (verse 18); "Why . . . do you submit to . . . rules?" (verse 20).

  3. Discuss what you think these commands mean.

  4. Because there is a "therefore" in verse 16, the reason for the first two commands are found in the previous verses (13-15). Discuss how these commands are based on those verses.

  5. Note that the reason for the last statement of what they are to avoid is found in verses 22-23. Discuss why you should not follow such ascetic, strict practices, based on these verses.

  6. Be sure to discuss how these three warnings of Paul are important to you today.

- *Continuing Through Colossians*

  You may choose to go through the rest of the book of Colossians observing together what you see and discussing the meaning of the verses. If so, we suggest you take the following portions each time: Colossians 3:1-11;

Colossians 3:12-17; Colossians 3:18—4:1; Colossians 4:2-6; Colossians 4:10-18.

- *Reading Together*

  Reading a book on any subject that expresses Christian truths and values can be a very valuable way to provoke discussions, especially about topics that may be sensitive and hard to talk about. Reading out loud about such topics can provoke some talk, or at least, it can give you that satisfaction of having considered the topic together. The following excerpt from *The House on the Rock*, a book about family life based on the Book of Proverbs that Chick wrote will provide an example of this kind of study.

- *Discussing a Topic*

  You may merely want to share what you think and believe about a topic. The following list of topics can be used for individual TWO-GETHER TIMES. Try a few of them.

  How does a Christian handle worry?

  How can we know the will of God?

  What do we fear and how should we handle it?

  How should we handle failure?

  What is our view of success and is it what it should be?

  How do we react to problems and how should we?

  What do you think about dying and do you fear it?

  What should a Christian think and do about people who may not have enough to eat?

What should a Christian do about some national or world problem?

What ethical problems do we face in the workplace and how should we handle them?

What are spiritual gifts and how can we know what ours are?

• *Using a Bible Dictionary*

Sometimes your discussion of a topic can be enhanced by simply consulting a Bible dictionary and reading that together. This should follow a discussion. For example, if you have been discussing death and dying, you could then read what a Bible dictionary says about the subject to get a biblical view. The following TWO-GETHER TIMES will give you a taste of this.

1. Discuss together what you think worry is and how a Christian should handle it.

2. Now, read the section about worry from a Bible dictionary.

3. Discuss what you have read and reflect on its helpfulness to you.

• *Using a Concordance or a Topical Bible*

This will usually take more time than you might want to spend. But, on the other hand, perhaps one of your TWO-GETHER TIMES discussions arouses special curiosity and interest in an answer to some questions you've raised: for example, you may wonder if the Bible makes a difference between concern and anxiety and whether or not Jesus' telling us not to worry means there is no such thing as legitimate concern. You could get some understanding of the Bible's view of anxiety by looking up the verses that deal with it; a concordance will list these verses. Note the verses and then discuss what you can learn from looking at all these references.

CHAPTER SIX

Growing Two-gether

"Encourage one another and build each other up."
—1 Thessalonians 5:11

Y̶ou don't do that anymore." These words from Ginger mean
so much to me. She's saying I no longer have an annoying
trait I had earlier in life. Granted, I still have some, along with
some new ones, but I have changed somewhat for the better since
we met. We both have. We've grown, individually and together.

And much of our maturing has come because of each other.
The Holy Spirit works that way; Hebrews 10:24 implies this. "And
let us consider how we may spur one another on toward love and
good deeds. Let us not give up meeting together." God wants us
to creatively ponder (the meaning of *consider*) how to provoke one
another to change, to do what one couple does: "We challenge and
motivate each other."

One of the major ways we grow is by a process called *integration.* "I keep all my business knowledge on one side of my head and
my Bible knowledge on the other," a man supposedly said, explaining how he managed being a Christian in the workplace. Someone
replied, "Shake your head, brother, and there will be a revolution."

This symbolic shaking of the head is integration. And it creates
pandemonium—in a good sense. We can never be quite sure of
what will happen if we truly accept Jesus' invitation: "Follow me."

Commercial fishermen were turned into earthshaking leaders, corrupt tax-collectors were changed into generous philanthropists, an adulterous women became a witness of the resurrected Christ.

The thrill, victory, and satisfaction of being a Christian occurs at the point where our Christian beliefs impact us practically where the rubber meets the road. Making truth relevant will put the most zest into your study. This is foremost in practicing any of the disciplines. Trivial, unimportant stuff won't stir our blood. Today we are so bombarded by information, we must pay attention to only some of it to keep our sanity. We can't afford the time and energy to notice everything that interests us; there is just too much of it pouring from the media. We've had to learn to select what we absorb; and we choose primarily on the basis of our needs, shrugging the rest off with, "Who needs it?" If we can't answer this question positively, we won't be motivated, stimulated, and benefited by our discussions. Studying is not the only step in growing spiritually, any more than chewing food is in physical growth. The nourishment must be digested and carried to every cell of our body. So, too, God and His Word must permeate our minds, feelings, and actions. Scripture repeatedly warns against harboring ideas in our heads that we never put to use.

The Apostle James is emphatic: "Do not merely listen to the word, and so deceive yourselves. Do what it says" (James 1:22). The blessing's in the doing, said Jesus: "Now that you know these things, you will be blessed if you do them" (John 13:17).

Scripture is meant to be lived, not just learned. By it, Paul says, we are "thoroughly equipped for every good work." To be equipped is to be in fit shape. In secular Greek literature the term is used of a boat that has two oars—an apt picture. The Christian who studies the Word without applying it has only one oar in the water.

To avoid paddling with only one oar we must refuse to separate our spirituality from the rest of life, which, unfortunately, we are sometimes encouraged to do. We've often heard this prayer at the beginning of a worship service: "Lord, help us to forget our cares and our worries and to concentrate on You." Actually, worshiping does not demand we forget our worries to ponder God's greatness but to concentrate on it in the light of our worries. A sick child, a grouchy boss, a financial setback, and other concerns are not to be left outside the church door but brought into God's presence where we can gain a true picture of them in the light of His greatness and grace.

Bible study that is not made relevant will soon become dull and lifeless, a drudgery. Our motivation to continually read and study it is sustained by the meaning, direction, and purpose it gives to our lives. Devoid of this, Bible study is reduced to a fishing expedition for facts and merely an academic exercise.

Just because the Bible is God's Word does not guarantee it will grip us like a good mystery or an interesting novel. This is especially true whenever we have already read much of it repeatedly so that most of the stories are as familiar as childhood fairy tales. The element of surprise or novelty is no longer left to keep our interest. So, once again reading about Nehemiah rebuilding the walls of Jerusalem, we may be thinking to ourselves, even with a tinge of guilt, "Who cares?" We already know how the story turns out and there are far more important things to be concerned about than fixing a broken-down wall more than 2,000 years ago. After all, winning a game of "Bible Trivia" is not adequate motivation to study Scripture.

But, getting a message from God is adequate motivation—one that will make a difference at work or in my marriage or will make me more emotionally stable or show me a way out of a dilemma or enable me to make a mark on the world. This is what caused the Psalmist to pray: "I delight in your decrees; I will not neglect your word." His was not the raving of a book critic over the literary style and finesse of a new novel. He was awed by the practicality as well as the beauty of Scripture. He sang of Scripture as something to "walk in," "observe," "keep," "do" and "trust in" (Psalm 119).

Interjecting the spiritual domain into life is what we call integration. It puts the spark into the other disciplines and therefore may be the most important of all. Although we've already said a great deal about relating spirituality to life in previous chapters, more remains to be said, particularly about guidelines for connecting what you study to daily life.

TWO TALK

- What do you now do together to integrate truth into your lives?

- Is this a weak or strong point of relating spiritually?

PROCEED FROM LIFE TO STUDY

Usually we think of Bible study going from truth to life. We interpret, then apply. But, it's just as important to sometimes move in the other direction: from life to truth. Said one couple: "Our time together is often for discussion. We can do this by starting with an issue of life and then going to Scripture for an answer." Another reported: "We talk about theological or biblical implications of current events. Sometimes we can start with the 'spiritual,' a Bible passage, and then reflect about how it shapes what we do and think."

It's sort of like getting sugar into our tea; sometimes we pour the tea first, then add the sugar; other times, we put the sugar in the cup and then pour the tea; the end result is the same: a mixture. A husband reported how he and his wife use both approaches.

> Our time together is often for discussion. It is generally triggered by one of three things and these shape the form and content of our discussion. First, we sometimes discuss a book or passage of Scripture that we have read and that seems particularly relevant. Second, we sometimes discuss an issue that springs from a question of my wife at her work. Third, we sometimes discuss theological and biblical implications of current events. How our faith informs us on issues from affirmative action to xenophobia.

What you do makes sense since what you study will be interesting if you start with what you are interested in. It also makes study purposeful since you have an idea of what you are looking for, like when you are shopping. You save time when you enter the shopping mall knowing what you're looking for instead of wandering around till you find something you need.

There are many ways couples can start with life and go to spiritual resources. Like the couple mentioned earlier, they can be alert to problems, questions, and issues that crop up in everyday life: a telephone solicitation for funds, a problem with a child, a crisis at work, a struggle with temper, etc. In their efforts to deal with these, they can discuss what their Christian faith contributes. They can do it informally, while riding in their car or lying in bed after the kids have gone to bed. Integration can be done in bits and pieces, snatching a moment here and there.

Or, you can be more formal about it by brainstorming the problems, questions, and issues each is facing and then planning devotional times to tackle them, selecting appropriate Scriptures to study and discuss. If you're under a lot of stress, read Psalms; at a time of loss, study a book about grief; in need of a spiritual jolt, try one of the Old Testament prophets. Choose books or cassette tapes that fit your present situation. Newly married couples can learn about Christian marriage by reading aloud from books, listening to cassettes, or watching videos on the subject. If conflict has you frustrated, your devotional time can be used to study how to handle it. Devotional times don't have to be lengthy; just ten minutes at a time with a book or video can add up to a lot of learning and discussion.

Being flexible about the topics for your devotional times is another way to cut a path from life to truth. You can scrap your plans any time to discuss some issue that has come up. If one of you faces a crisis on the job, or you're perplexed about your child, or you're faced with a decision, skip the passage of Scripture you intended to study and talk and pray about the issue at hand.

Merging God's truth and our life—that's our goal. Moving

from life issues to that truth is a highly effective means for doing that. But the reverse, going from God's Word to life, is just as effective, especially when you put into practice the following steps.

TWO TALK

- What problem did you have recently that you deliberately tried to use spiritual resources to find an answer to?

- Is there any way you can better identify problems and issues in order to study about them together?

IDENTIFY A PRINCIPLE OF SCRIPTURE

Applying the Bible isn't just a matter of taking a verse of Scripture and putting it into action. To do so would be quite absurd. That Jesus told a rich man to sell his things and give money to the poor doesn't demand we do the same. Nor should we eat locusts because John the Baptist did. Or as mentioned in the last chapter, because God outlawed some of Eden's fruit, He wasn't putting restrictions on all gardens.

Yet, in all of these Scriptures, there's a message for us: It's in the principles. The word to the rich fellow to sell everything and give to the poor really wasn't about helping the poor; it was about worshiping money. Jesus was trying to show the man that he was putting his wealth before God. That's the principle for us, and it's stated elsewhere in Scripture: "Keep your lives free from the love of money" (Hebrews 13:5). Now we have something to work with. We're probably not in a position to sell all and give it away, but we are able to be cautious about loving money. That we can apply: working too many hours to buy luxuries and neglecting service for Christ; being too tight to give to the church building fund; too busy thinking about earning and investing to spend time with God.

Even John the Baptist's diet of insects can teach us something:

that serving God sometimes requires accepting austere conditions. And the principle from the command about the center tree in the Garden of Eden is clear enough: listen to God or else.

A principle is a broadly stated guideline, like "Be kind to one another." Kindness is an abstract idea that can be expressed in thousands of particular ways. We smile at little kids who mouth words they don't seem to understand: "Be kind to one another" a three-year-old boy recites in Sunday school while clobbering a little red-headed girl. Doing this doesn't indicate that he doesn't know anything about the word *kind*. Rather, he hasn't yet learned all that it means. So far, he's learned that it means share your cookies, take turns at the playground swings, etc. In a moment, the teacher will teach him that it also means you don't do certain things to sweet little redheads. And when he is much older, he'll understand the word *kind* as an abstract concept that he can apply to new situations.

Sometimes the principles of the Bible are clear because they are stated as principles, like the command to be kind. Books in the New Testament that are in the form of letters contain a lot of them. "Husbands, love your wives as Christ loved the church," "Live in harmony," or "Offer your bodies as living sacrifices." Note, they aren't very specific: for example, exactly what you should do Monday morning to offer your body isn't clearly spelled out. And some principles are narrower than others. The command to love one another is quite broad. However, chapter 13 of 1 Corinthians narrows the meaning: love is being patient, not rude, not easily angered, etc. Note, however, that even these narrower ideas are still principles. We are left to determine exactly what specific rudeness to avoid or how patience is fleshed out.

At other times, principles in Scripture are not so easy to identify. In some instances we have to go from the particular to the general, especially when applying historical passages. What King David did, for example, in a particular situation must be turned into a principle we can apply to ourselves. Sometimes the message is obvious: Trying to avoid exposure of his adulterous affair with the pregnant Bathsheba, he arranged for the death of her husband. This clearly tells us what we should not do. Though we might not have the power to have a man killed by having him ordered to the front line of battle, we get the message that murder is wrong and horrendous.

But, the particular actions of biblical characters do not always translate so easily into principles for our lives. Does David and Jonathan's close friendship suggest in principle every man should have such a friend? Do Abraham and Sarah's several quarrels suggest it's okay for husbands and wives to have conflict? The miracles of Elijah—should we expect to see them today?

Even the record of God's actions are not always easily turned into principles. Does God speak to us in dreams as He once did? Does He refrain from punishing nations if there are enough righteous people as was the case in Abraham's time?

How we answer such questions is a crucial issue, especially, as we saw in the previous chapter, since acting on a wrong principle can be disastrous, as it was for a sick toddler. We should be careful to have a legitimate principle, following the suggestions of the last chapter. In addition, before we bank our lives on one, we should consult some commentaries or ask a reliable pastor or Bible teacher to confirm it.

TWO TALK

- Do you agree that we need to find the principle of a passage in order to apply it?

- Is it difficult for you to find the principle in a passage of Scripture?

MAKE SPECIFIC APPLICATION TO YOUR LIFE

Application doesn't end with finding the principle and believing it. We need to ponder how it specifically applies to our life. We need to ask, what does this command, truth, promise, example, word of encouragement, or warning mean to me right here and now. When we get down to the nitty-gritty like this, we put God's truth on a collision course with our reality. The impact will be fierce but the rewards life-changing. Otherwise, Bible study amounts to grasping principles that don't grab us.

Take the previous example, "Be kind to one another." To apply it requires not only asking, "What does it mean to be kind in a relationship?" but asking even more specifically, "What does it mean to be kind in a husband and wife relationship?" Now, we can get specific: What does kindness have to do with sex, speaking, household chores, listening, shopping, etc.?

The broader the principle, the more difficult it is to get specific. But, even narrower ones require a bit of effort to make them useful. It demands our asking a lot of questions about different areas of our lives: What does it mean to be patient? Does it have anything to do with being stuck in rush-hour traffic, or when your husband is late, or when your wife forgot to buy sugar, etc.?

Principles from the lives of Bible characters can also be difficult to apply since, as we've suggested, we can't always be sure that we should follow their example. But in most cases we can. We can emulate Abraham's faith, David's love for God, or Joshua's courage. To apply the lesson from the example, we can try to think of parallel situations. Though we may not be facing giant enemies in battle, we may have people or problems that scare us. Looking at how Joshua faced his fear can mean something to us. Or take Nehemiah, the wall-builder. Though we don't have to organize a nation to fortify a city, we do have "building projects," (things we are trying to accomplish). And we face setbacks, opposition, discouragement in our enterprises just as he did. We need to ask, what can we learn from him about this area of our life?

About now you're ready for an example. Let's take one from Nehemiah. He's easy to identify with since his life was like most of ours, one challenge after another. He led the Jews in rebuilding Jerusalem's wall to give them protection after they were once again in their land, after being held captive in Babylon. Unless they survive as a nation in that place, Jesus could not be born there about 400 years later. Nehemiah's task isn't easy since building the huge wall is arduous, and Israel's nearby enemies oppose it. Their resistance peaks as the story is told in Chapter four of Nehemiah.

There's little difficulty in identifying the theme of this passage. It recounts how Arabs and Ammonites and others try to prevent the Jews from completing their wall. But the emphasis is mostly on how Nehemiah and the people deal with this opposition. So now we have discerned the theme: facing opposition.

We're now ready to look for how they did this. It's not hard to find a number of tactics, which we'll list here.

1. When they ridiculed, Nehemiah prayed. "Hear us, O our God for we are despised. Turn their insults back on their own heads" (4:4).

2. When they threatened to attack them, Nehemiah prayed and prepared for it: "We prayed to our God and posted a guard day and night to meet this threat" (4:9).

3. When there were continued threats and rumors of possible attacks, they "continued the work with half the men holding spears" (4:21).

Now, you say, that's fine; the next time we're building a wall and someone threatens military action against us, we'll know what to do. What does this have to do with us right now?

To answer that, you have to formulate principles; in this case, we have to go from the concrete responses of Nehemiah to some more general ideas. Here's how.

1. To face ridicule, pray about it.

2. To face threat of opposition, be on the alert and do something about it.

3. To face continued threat, stay on the alert, but don't let it stop you from doing what you're doing with your life.

Now we are ready to apply these principles. It's easiest to

apply them to situations where people oppose you. So, you have to ponder if and where you are facing such resistance. Maybe you're not physically threatened, but you may have someone at work that is out to get you. Or, perhaps you're facing some stiff opposition to your faith in Christ. Your first tactic is to pray; that's obvious enough. A man told us recently that when he was under vicious attack from a superior after his company changed hands, it took him quite a while to decide to do that. Then every day he prayed for the man, often more than once. Months later, the person was fired. This was not what he had prayed for, but he confessed he was relieved. Unfortunately, the woman who replaced his superior was just as fierce. So he prayed for her. She too was fired later, and he was vindicated.

But the passage tells us to do more than pray, and that's important. "We prayed to God and we posted a guard" is a pretty significant statement. Some might accuse him of lacking faith, since they believe prayer would have been enough. Holding up traffic, his car broken down, a Christian leader wrote about how he trusted God in the situation. While common sense suggested he and his friends do something about it, he claimed he did the faith thing: "We didn't get out and push; we praised." Midst blaring horns and angry motorists, they sat and prayed until a mechanic, who was passing by, rapped on the window and offered to help. Apparently Nehemiah would disagree with this tactic. He'd pray, then push. And other Scripture confirms that it's okay to put legs on our prayers.

The third principle is just as insightful. We shouldn't let opposition paralyze us. Sometimes we must defend ourselves, but we shouldn't let that distract us from doing our job.

Now we have some principles to apply to our situation, and they are dynamite. However, you may still object: You don't really have any big-time opposition in your life right now. *How can we apply this to our lives?* you ask.

Simply broaden the application. Ask, *What do I face in life that is similar to opposition?* There are any number of answers: difficulties, problems, temptations, addictions, etc. This passage can speak to any of these. Take, for example, some personal problem. First, pray about it. Second, do something about it if you can. Many people don't: They pray about a problem with their child, marriage, church, or community, but they don't do anything about it. Don't let prayer be a substitute for action. Then, while you're dealing with the problem, keep on doing something constructive with your life. Don't let personal struggles make you give up teaching Sunday school or being a youth leader, etc. All this insight for living comes from one brief chapter of Scripture.

Remember, too, to apply Scripture to your thought life.

Recently, Christian leaders have been using a new phrase: "Think Christianly." By it, they simply mean that God's truth should rule our thoughts as well as our behavior. This requires not only the acquisition of new ideas but the discarding of old ones. This, too, is integration—a most important form of it, since it strikes at the source of our behavior, the mind. What we think largely determines what we do. Though personal change is caused by many factors, the renewal of the mind is clearly one of them and perhaps the most important (Romans 12:2).

God's Word is like a mental detergent, washing the mind's grime and grit, which can be extremely damaging to our well-being.

"Sex is for animals," a wife said to her husband, explaining why she wasn't interested in it and why he shouldn't be either. Shaped by certain negative biblical statements about improper sex, her attitude was wrong, but it was punishing her husband. Wrong ideas give birth to shame, guilt, and anxiety: Christians should not fail; Godly people will prosper financially; Sickness is a punishment for being bad.

Sometimes we may know the truth but not fully assimilate it into our hearts. Then, we must do some things to permit God's word to touch us deeply. By discussing these, couples can help each other overcome negative thoughts and attitudes.

Imagine the help you can give to each other as you try ferreting out principles of wisdom from Scripture and build your living and your thinking on them. To get specific also requires something more. If you are going to build a bridge between God's truth and yourself, you have to not only know God's truth but know yourself.

TWO TALK

- Does this practice of applying a principle to life seem difficult?

- Exactly how is it difficult for you?

- How can you do more of this together?

ATTEMPT TO KNOW YOURSELF

The Apostle James compares listening to God's Word to looking in a mirror (James 1:24). His point is that Scripture gives us a picture of our true self, and if we are going to change, we must not forget it. To apply Scripture to ourselves requires knowing ourselves. People can be angry or impatient and not realize it. They feel no need for what the Bible says about these emotions. Jesus noted this human tendency to ignore the plank in our own eye while quickly spotting the speck in someone else's.

Admitting to ourselves that we have problems is difficult to do. Shying away from the truth about ourselves protects us from the shock of being exposed too suddenly to our darker, weaker side. Denial is a way of defending ourselves, of maintaining self-respect despite our blemishes and flaws, protecting us from the pain of seeing our defects, and relieving us from the need to deal with them. It takes many forms.

Sometimes persons in denial are totally blind to their fault, though everyone around them sees it clearly. A woman recently described a husband like this. She once told him he was just like his mother (meaning he possessed some of her bad traits). He became so violently angry, she was afraid to ever mention it again.

Diminishing the problem is another approach to denial. More subtle than blindness, it expresses itself in phrases like: "My anger isn't that bad" or "I'm not that selfish." In this case, we suspect we have a problem, but it's not serious enough to harm anybody or take pains to do something about it. Often this type of denial resorts to comparisons—"I'm certainly not as insensitive as Hank." Delay is another form of denial, possibly the most deadly. We admit the problem but put off solving it. Its favorite tactic is making promises: "When work slows down, I'll start an exercise program," or making pious statements: "We ought to start praying more together," or making excuses: "I can't take the time to face that now."

Denial isn't all bad; too clear a look at ourselves could plunge us into depression. Sometimes we do need to protect ourselves from ourselves; yet we can defend ourselves too much for too long. Many in Jesus' day refused His remedies because they denied their need for them. To them He said, "It is not the healthy who need a doctor, but the sick."

Recognizing why we may have a severe tendency to deny may help us overcome it, since some of us are more prone to it than others. People from dysfunctional families are particularly susceptible because these families specialized in it. Members of such families sometimes aren't aware of how abnormal their behavior is. Children are taught to deal with problems by excusing them or explaining them away. They were told, "Daddy only said those things because he was drunk." The implied message is that it was okay for him to do that. Or, "Dad only broke my arm this time; he's not so bad." Or, Dad excuses his wife's abusing the children by telling them, "Mommy only got angry because she's not feeling well." Denial like that is contagious. People who grow up in homes where it's practiced continue to do it long after they've left them.

Shame and guilt can sometimes keep us from seeing ourselves. We cover up and lie to ourselves rather than face these two powerful emotions. Hopelessness, too, can blind us. Feeling unable to do anything about a problem, we simply ignore it. This, too, has its roots in our past. Bucking up against insurmountable family problems, we learned as children to feel helpless. Unable to face and to solve problems, we coped by escaping from them.

Nothing helps us get a true glimpse of ourselves like a view of God's grace. God's warm love and forgiveness is like sunlight to a flower. It enables us to open ourselves up to Him, to honestly expose who we are to Him. Knowing His grace is sufficient to absolve our most depraved thoughts, feelings, or actions enables us to be honest, to confess our sins.

Couples who lavish that same warm grace upon one another will provide a climate for overcoming denial. Yet, as we mentioned in dealing with confession, couples are not always in the best place to help one another be honest. They are a threat to honesty at times because their failures and immaturities often hurt and distress their spouse. Therefore, they are not merely in a position to say, "I have done wrong," but, "I have done wrong to you." And that is obviously more difficult to say.

But, couples can help each other acquire self-knowledge. Marriage makes you look hard at yourself. Adjusting to each other exposes your differences and faults. When forced to change, you feel torn, twisted, and pounded into a different person. In the process you can learn a great deal about yourself if you're open to it.

Because you know each other so well you can serve as valuable mirrors to one another. Most couples today are best friends and even serve as each other's analysts. Becky, for example, uses questions to help her husband, Wayne, understand himself. "If he appears to be angry, I, of course, have to ask him why, since he might be feeling upset with me. Often," she continues, "he doesn't know exactly what he's feeling. So, I go into my question routine. Is it something I said or did? Is it something with the kids? If his feeling isn't related to us, I start getting into some of his deep personal things. Is it related to something that happened in his past? Has it anything to do with his dad? Wayne really appreciates this. He's not the kind of person who will sit down and say, 'Let's talk about my feelings.' But when I challenge him to speak up whenever I sense something's wrong, he responds. He's much better at identifying his emotions now and even beginning to tell us how he's feeling."

We can also analyze one another when discussing Scripture. Reading a passage about people, we can ask each other: "Are you like Abraham?" or "Would you have acted like Sarah?" or "Do you see yourself in Peter?" If the passage is emotionally charged, we can explore how we are accustomed to feeling. After reading the Psalmist's lament: "My soul is downcast within me," ask, "When have you felt that way?" A question is the most effective tool to apply any passage of Scripture or page of a book to our lives. Simply ask, "How do you relate to this idea, person or story?"

It helps if you direct your questions and application to specific areas of your life. See yourself as pieces of PIES: physical, intellectual, emotional, social and spiritual and apply a principle of Scripture to these sections of yourself. For example, ask, "What does the phrase: 'Be anxious for nothing,' mean to each of us?" "Do I most worry about my body, my thought life, my feelings, others or my walk with God?" By this you can sort out the major area of your worries and get a better glimpse of and better hold on yourself.

Let's also help each other discover our bright side by including affirmation in your application of Scripture. Often, we are so critical of ourselves that we are blind to our own virtues or to how God has worked in our lives.

At times we need others to tell us they see us progressing in an area of struggle or see us strong where we think we are weak, and husbands and wives are in such a good position to do so. Provide some feedback. Say things like: "You are much like Joshua here; I see you as very brave." "This passage about love reminds me of the unselfish way you give of yourself to others." "I see more patience in your life than ever." Follow Paul's advice: "Encourage one another and build each other up" (1 Thessalonians 5:11).

TWO TALK

- Is it difficult for your to see yourself as you really are?

- Are you open to your partner helping you understand yourself?

- How can your partner help you know better who you are?

BE POSITIVE AS WELL AS NEGATIVE

Just as in constructing a house, building each other up requires more than tearing things down. Granted, personal maturing, like construction does require some demolishing and some altering. The Bible contains plenty of negatives—the word *not* being in nine of the Ten Commandments. Yet, to build, we have to add new structure, replace what's been torn down.

Tennis teachers suggest you improve your stroke by concentrating on what you ought to be doing rather than what you shouldn't be. For example, it is better to say to yourself. "Keep my wrist straight" rather than, "Don't bend my wrist." If you focus on not bending, your subconscious may fix on the bending, causing you to do what you are trying not to.

This seems to be true in other areas of life. If we focus on what we shouldn't do, we may be tempted to do it. A dieter who continually tells himself, "Don't eat Big Macs" constantly reminds himself of "two all beef patties, special sauce, lettuce, cheese, pickles, onions, etc." This idea lies behind the joke about the elderly woman who complained that the Ten Commandments shouldn't be mentioned in church because they might give people ideas.

But, of course, we should read them—as well as all the Bible's other warnings about what we should not do. But we should also concentrate on what we should do.

Recovering alcoholics practice this. They know that they must not merely quit drinking; they must do something else instead. Instead of hanging out in the bar or drinking themselves to sleep at night, recovering alcoholics know they must find something else to do with their time. We can use this approach to change any of our behaviors: Just concentrate on what you should be doing when you are doing what you shouldn't be.

The Apostle Paul seems to suggest this. In his epistle to the Colossians he gives both negative and positive commands, seeming to use the analogy of changing clothes. Christians should put off certain sins but, at the same time, put on virtue. Sexual immorality is to be replaced by love, hatred by kindness, etc.

To facilitate change we should ask ourselves, "What is the opposite of the trait I'm trying to get rid of?" For example, if I'm angry and impatient in heavy traffic and I want to change, I shouldn't simply try not to be upset. Not being upset doesn't give me a picture or a goal of what to strive for. I must determine what that is and center my energies on being that way. Keep reminding each other to ask what we should be doing, not just what should we not be doing. This will give you something to aim for and will help you move to the next step in integrating God's truth into your lives.

TWO TALK

- Do you have an example when you have tried to change some negative in your life by trying to do the opposite? How has it worked?

- Is there a problem you have now that you can let your partner help you decide on some positive action to deal with it?

SET GOALS AND MAKE SPECIFIC PLANS

Use your TWO-GETHER TIMES to identify specific goals for your lives and to make plans to reach them. At such times, try finishing your devotionals with more than a vague idea of what you ought to do. If you both feel you should be more hospitable, discuss how and when and with whom. Establish some concrete objectives: perhaps to invite a couple and a single person from your church for dinner one night a month or to regularly volunteer to house the church's visiting speakers. Then, put these things into your schedule.

Sometimes your goals may be quite modest. But a small step in the right direction is better than staying where you are.

TWO TALK

- When have you successfully, as a couple, set goals and worked out a plan to schieve them?

- Has this worked well?

- How can you improve doing this?

SUPPORT EACH OTHER

The statement, "You can't be a Christian alone" makes a lot of sense. Being a Christian includes loving and caring for others. It also involves being loved and supported by others. As we said earlier, we need each other to help us grow.

This is partly true because it's not easy to change. The superintendent of a local high school once joked, "Sometimes my teenage daughter asks, 'Dad, may I go out tonight?' To answer her, I think through all I learned in my adolescent psychology courses, then I sift through ideas from my secondary education course, then I run through data from my Ph.D. management courses, and I confidently reply: 'Go ask your mother.'" It's tough to get truth from our head to our habit.

To change we need determination, motivation, and discipline. While the Holy Spirit can generate these from inside us, He can also prompt them through others outside us. Being so heavily involved in each others' lives, husbands and wives can, by God's power, support each other in their efforts to grow in Christ.

Yet, being married can make it hard to foster change in your partner. Adjusting to each other sometimes requires so much change that we often feel our partner is unduly pressuring us. The early years especially demand torturous revisions of thinking, attitudes, and habits, making us feel like a house torn apart and remodeled floor by floor. This is fine. We know it has to happen, but it's not fun. To live with each other, one of us has to give. The problem is, each often feels we are doing all the giving, thinking: "For a change, why don't you change?"

Under pressure to move, we often don't, resisting like mules. We treat each other like stubborn animals and turn to the time-honored practices of yelling, screaming, begging, threatening, pouting, and—the most popular of all—nagging. Christians sometimes marshall their spiritual forces to jostle a spouse in the right direction— talk to the pastor, read this book, go to this meeting, etc. Spiritual times together become opportunities to hint at the problem and turn up the heat. We play ecclesiastical basketball. God tosses a message to us. Ignoring it for ourselves, we quickly pass it to our spouse. I've often kidded Ginger when she would ask, "What passage shall we read today?" "Ephesians 5, about wives submitting to their husbands," I suggest. "Fine," she replies, "just so we get to the part about husbands loving their wives." This little joshing game illustrates what couples play out day after day; only often it is gravely serious. Hearing a sermon or reading a passage of Scripture together, a man thinks to himself, "I sure hope she got that." She knows what's going on since she's aware of the problem and that he's aware, and she feels squeezed in a marital vise. Couples soon discover these pressure tactics work extremely well. They dramatically produce change—in our relationship. We withdraw from each other disillusioned, disappointed, and often angry. In our attempts to remodel one another, we have demolished our marriage. Some separate. Some stay together but have little contact. If they do, it is often abusive.

Those who successfully survive these years of adjustment do so by patiently accepting each other. They also focus on changing themselves, not their partners. Otherwise they get locked into codependency, an overdependence on each other that actually prevents each of us from growing. There are ways to combat this.

Don't demand too much

Watch what you demand of each other. Don't demand too much or to do it where you have no right to. In the name of *accountability* a husband insisted that his wife report regularly about whether she were: 1) staying on her diet, 2) following her exercise plan, 3) having her personal devotions. Needless to say, when she came to Chick for counseling she said she felt a bit "boxed in." After all, she had lived alone for ten years after leaving home without reporting to anybody and had done quite well with her health and spiritual life.

"Let me talk to him," Chick suggested, confident, since the husband was a seminary student, he would readily take the advice of one of his professors. He didn't. He argued that he should treat his wife the way he and several of his Christian buddies treated each other. They had made a pact to hold each other accountable for what they did. He was simply doing the same with his wife. Chick tried to explain that marriage was different than his group of Christian friends.

Not only did he hold his ground, he tightened the grip. Some time after he and his wife moved away from school, she called to say he was also limiting her phone calls and rationing the minutes she spent with friends. When Chick mentioned the situation to a Christian counselor on our faculty, he blustered, "That's wife abuse."

This is not to say that it's always abusive to make demands on one another. Being married means you are responsible to one another in certain areas. We have every right to suggest, and even insist on, changes that affect our relationship. A husband can insist his wife not flirt with other men and a wife that her husband not neglect her. And sometimes when our partner gets addicted to drugs or alcohol or is caught in some obsession, we have to confront them, sometimes harshly.

But we must constantly be asking, "Is this an issue that is personal to my spouse or is it one that is within the bounds of our marriage?" Codependency has to do with boundaries. To intrude into your spouse's personal boundaries can be extremely oppressive. A husband, for example, might insist his wife not chew gum. Now, it's his right to ask her not to whenever they are kissing; that involves both of them (and he might not want to risk ending up with it), but chewing gum privately is her business. However, you could argue that he's only trying to avoid what gum with sugar in it might do to her teeth and that is his business. The same thing could be true of eating too much, which is a hazard to health.

Yet some things can't be controlled from the outside. Change must come from the inside out. Unless you have absolute control over someone, you cannot make them stop drinking or eat properly. As long as you keep on pushing them, they may refuse to push themselves. If you keep pressure on from the outside, then they don't turn it on in the inside.

We have to avoid needlessly intruding on our partner's personal life, even when we disagree with what they are doing. We have to give each other freedom to fail, respecting each other's choices. This liberates people to be responsible for the changes they need to make. Chick explained this once during a Friday evening meeting in a weekend seminar in a New England city. On Saturday afternoon a woman reported to him she had followed his suggestion. For years she had been complaining to her husband about how he dressed, jeans and sometimes dirty shirts—something she would never do in public. Walking beside him embarrassed her, which she's been forcefully telling him for twenty years.

"This morning," she said, "I told him I would never again gripe about how he dressed. After dropping his jaw, he asked me to repeat myself. I did. Later, he went out and bought two new shirts and two new trousers and dressed very nicely to come to the seminar this afternoon."

We don't like marriage to take away our personal liberty. When someone robs us of our space, we fight to gain it back. Apparently this is what this husband was doing. When the pressure was off, he felt free to choose for himself.

Don't do too much

We should also avoid doing too much for our spouse. Codependents like to say, "Here, let me do it." Demanding can be a way of doing that, saying, "I'll be your conscience. I'll keep reminding you. I'll take charge." Rescuing people from the consequences of their actions is another way to do more than we should. People married to alcoholics do this. They cover up by lying to the boss when their hungover partner is unable to report for work. This is similar to the wife of a workaholic making excuses to her children for his neglect of them. As long as we rescue and protect them, they will not feel the pressure to change and they will fail to solve their problem. Proverbs 19:19 makes this clear: "An ill-tempered man must pay the penalty; if you rescue him you will have to do it again."

The same thing is true when we try to solve our partner's problems for them by doing all sorts of things: telling them what to do, constantly reminding them of it, and ever putting pressure on them. Essentially, we try to be their conscience, guide, and willpower. We become their substitute. So, as long as we're playing the game for them, they sit on the bench, stuck in their problem, resisting our efforts. Essentially we perpetuate the problem when we try to stop drinking, eating, gambling for someone. Certainly, the Bible says: "Carry each other's burdens, and in this way you will fulfill the law of Christ" (Galatians 6:2). Yet, a few sentences later it warns: "Each one shall bear his own load" (Galatians 6:5, *New American Standard Bible*). The different Greek words used for "burdens" and "load" explains the difference.

Burdens are like rocks too heavy for one person to handle. At times, troubles are such that we need others to help by giving us a lift. The load is like a backpack, representing what we ourselves are personally responsible for carrying. When we take someone else's assigned backpack, we rob them of the opportunity to solve their own problem and do their own thing. Love means doing what's best for someone. Sometimes that requires refusing to help.

Instead of refusing to substitute for their efforts, we can best help them by offering our support. In essence, our attitude toward each other should be: "I won't try to fix you, but I'll support you in fixing yourself." This means we'll suggest steps for solving the problem, but we'll let our partner take them. At times, we'll suggest options but refrain from giving advice.

Instead of preventing them from falling, we'll encourage them to pick themselves up after they have. Essentially, we'll stand on the sideline cheering, "You can do it," while refusing to do it for them.

Don't depend too much

Just as you can encourage a person to depend too much, you can easily depend too much on them. We do this in petty, sometimes amusing ways. "Remind me to buy milk on the way home from church tonight, will you, or we won't have any for breakfast in the morning." When you both forget, you accuse, "I told you to remind me." It's possible that requesting your partner to remember caused you to forget, because in your unconscious you had relieved yourself of the pressure to remember.

That leaning on your spouse caused you to have eggs instead of cereal for breakfast is no big deal, but such overdependence in other matters can be: when you trust someone else to break your bad habit, keep your spending or eating under control, think for you, etc. By doing so you may stifle your growth and remain stuck in the problem you won't face yourself. In the meantime, your partner, too, is stuck—in the frustration and disappointment that comes to those who try to force someone to change.

An ancient Chinese tale speaks to this. A father came into the house carrying several cornstalks, their roots dangling. His son asked him what he had been doing. "I have been out in the field helping them grow by pulling on them," his father replied. The story is rather foolish, but the lesson is profound. We cannot force plants nor people to grow. Nagging, jerking, and pressuring doesn't seem to work.

TWO TALK

- Is there an area where you demand too much, do too much, or depend too much on your partner?

- What problems does this create? How can you avoid doing this?

CONCLUSION

Don't insist, encourage. Your trust in God will enable you to do this. Committing our partner to God and His control relieves us of the need to control our spouse ourself. By faith we believe He is at work in us and that we grow from the inside out. Your practice of all the spiritual disciplines contributes to this. Worshiping keeps you focused on the reason for growing: God's glory. Celebrating fosters a positive attitude. Praying provides power. Studying supplies direction. And integrating makes us ever new.

Standing by someone you love, hand in hand, supporting them and watching them mature is one of life's—and marriage's—greatest experiences. It has been for us. Looking back at ourselves decades ago makes us cringe. We were so immature, often misunderstanding each other and failing God and others. Not that we're all wise and all right today, but we've come a long way. And it's because we brought God into our marriage and tried to treat each other as He treats us, except, of course, judg-

ing; that we leave to Him as Jesus said we should. His uncondi-
tional acceptance of us we've passed on to each other. As He's
forgiven us our failures, we've forgiven each other. And we've
tried to listen to each other as He does to us. We've trusted His
power and drew strength from one another, cried out to Him
and wept in each others arms. God loved us and we've tried to
love Him and each other—that, more than anything, summa-
rizes our marriage. We have been spiritually together. We pray
you will be, too.

TWO-GETHER
TIMES

• *Getting the Main Theme of a Passage and Applying It*

This TWO-GETHER TIMES is much like the previous
TWO-GETHER TIMES where you observed and discussed
the meaning of a passage of Scripture. The difference here
is that you are especially going to look for a major theme
and then discuss how it applies to your life.

1. Read aloud Psalm 23 with the idea of discovering the
main theme of the Psalm (we are beginning with an easy
one to demonstrate; however, expect a blessing).

2. Now, try to list all that the Psalm says about this theme,
making as many points as you can.

3. Discuss now which of those items (of God's care) you
most need right now.

4. Discuss how you believe God can give you what you
need (how will it come and from where, etc.).

5. Each pray that God the Shepherd will provide what the
other needs.

- *Getting the Main Theme of a Passage and Applying It*

  1. Read 2 Corinthians 12:1-10 with the idea of determining what you think is the main theme.

  2. Now list all that the passage says about that topic (in order to demonstrate to you this method, we will suggest that the main theme is *Paul's attitude toward his weaknesses.* List all that Paul says about this. For example, he "delights in weaknesses," verse 10.

  3. Now each of you share a weakness or two that you realize you have (point out your own, not each other's).

  4. Now discuss, point by point, whether you have the same attitude toward these weaknesses that Paul had.

  5. Talk about how you could change your attitude if you need to.

  6. Pray about matters raised in your discussion.

- *Getting the Main Theme of a Passage and Applying It*

  1. Read Hebrews 11:17-31 to discover the main theme.

  2. List each idea related to that theme. In this case, try to determine how each person acted in faith (for example: Moses' parents overcame fear; Rahab welcomed spies).

  3. Now try to determine the principle expressed in each case. For example, what did Rahab's welcoming the spies exemplify as a principle of faith or what principle of faith was involved in the people's marching around the wall of Jericho? Note: It's not really easy to see the principle in some of these cases.

  4. Each of you try to identify a situation in your life right now that calls for faith that is similar to one of the cases

in this passage. (For example, you fear what might happen at work if you are honest as God wants you to be.)

5. Pray for each other to have faith in your situation.

- *Using a Passage of Scripture to Affirm and Support One Another*

  1. Read the list of the fruit of the Spirit found in Galatians 5:22-23.

  2. Tell each other which one of these you most see in your partner.

  3. Now, each of you share which of these you would like to see more of in your life and why.

  4. Praise God for what you see of the Spirit's fruit in each other and pray for each other in your area of need.

- *Identifying with Persons of Scripture*

  Since much of the Bible consists of stories of people, we can learn from the example of others in these stories. Because they are so concrete and human, they are easy to identify with and seek to follow, when the example is positive. This amounts to using them as case studies, a method you have probably done at school or at church.

  1. Read aloud about the call of Abram in Genesis 12:1-9.

  2. Discuss how you would have felt if you had been Abram.

  3. Discuss why it would have been difficult for him to obey God or why it would not have been difficult.

  4. Discuss whether or not you have ever felt like Abraham in your life.

5. Discuss whether or not there is anything that you believe God wants you to do that requires the kind of faith Abraham showed here.

6. Pray for each other.

- *Identifying with Persons of Scripture*

  1. Read out loud Numbers 13:21-14:4.

  2. Pick out all the characters described in this passage.

  3. Share with each other the characters you most identify yourselves with. The people? Caleb? Moses?

  4. Discuss why you might be like those you identify with.

  5. Is there any situation in your life that is similar to the situation in this passage of Scripture?

  6. Discuss how you might face it based on anything you might learn from the people in this passage of Scripture.

  7. Pray about your situations and your reaction.

- *Identifying with a Person of Scripture*

  1. Read aloud the account of Peter's denial of Jesus in Matthew 26:31-35 and 26:69-75, thinking as you read about how you would or would not have been like Peter.

  2. Share with each other how you think Peter felt when Jesus told him he would disown Him.

  3. Share with each other how Peter must have felt when the servant girl pointed him out as a follower of Jesus.

  4. Share with each other whether you have felt like Peter on any occasion.

5. Discuss whether or not there is a situation where you are challenged to stand for Jesus and how you feel about it.

6. Talk about how you can avoid disowning Jesus in difficult situations.

7. Pray for each other.

- *Evaluating Your Spiritual Life and Helping Each Other Find a Plan for Improvement*

  1. Share with each other what areas of your life (or your spiritual life) that you would most like to improve.

  2. Tell each other what you think you might do to improve.

  3. Each of you react to what you partner has shared.

  4. Pray for each other.

- *Evaluating Your Emotional Life and Helping Each Other Find Solutions*

  1. Looking over the following list of emotions, each of you share what emotions are most problematic.

Sadness (depression)	Love, tenderness
Joy	Guilt
Anxiety, fear	Shame
Anger	Jealousy

  2. Explain to each other what you need to do to improve this area of your emotional life.

  3. Help each other make a plan for improving.

  4. Pray for each other.

- *Evaluating Your Social Life and Helping Each Other*

   1. Look over the following list of areas of your social life and
   share with each other what areas you need to improve in
   as an individual or as a couple:

      > Relationships with friends
      > Relationships with relatives
      > Relationships at church
      > Relationships in the neighborhood
      > Relationships at work

   2. Talk about what you can do to improve or develop these
   relationships.

   3. Help each other make plans for improving that area.

- *Evaluating Your Intellectual Life and Helping Each
  Other Improve*

   1. Each share whether or not you have a need to improve
   your mental life. Are you getting enough intellectual
   stimulation, or is there an area that you would like to or
   need to study more?

   2. Discuss with each other how you might improve in this
   area.

   3. Discuss any possible plans for improvement.

   4. Pray for each other.

- *Evaluating the Physical Aspect of Your Life and Helping
  Each Other Improve*

   1. Each share how you are doing physically. Do not
   evaluate each other, but listen to each other's own
   evaluation.

2. Then tell your partner what you think you might do to meet any physical need you have.

3. Help each other make plans to do what needs to be done.

4. Pray for each other.

Additional Resources

DEVOTIONAL BOOKS FOR COUPLES

This Love We Share: Daily Devotions to Bring Wholeness to Your Marriage by Harry and Emily Griffith. Published by Tyndale House Publishers, Wheaton, Illinois, 1995.

Becoming Soul Mates: Cultivating Spiritual Intimacy in the Early Years of Marriage by Les and Leslie Parrott. Published by Zondervan Publishing House, Grand Rapids, Michigan, 1995.

Moments Together for Couples: Devotions for Drawing Near to God and One Another by Dennis and Babara Rainey. Published by Regal Books, Ventura, California, 1995.

Quiet Times for Couples: A Daily Devotional by H. Norman Wright. Published by Harvest House Publishers, Eugene, Oregon, 1990.

15 Minutes to Build a Stronger Marriage: Weekly Togetherness for Busy Couples by Myron and Bobbie Yagel. Published by Tyndale House Publishers, Wheaton, Illinois, 1995.

STANDARD DEVOTIONAL BOOKS

My Utmost for His Highest: The Golden Book of Oswald Chambers, edited by James Reimann. Published by Discovery House Publishers, Grand Rapids, Michigan, 1995.

Celebration of Discipline by Richard J. Foster. Published by Harper and Row, New York, New York, 1978.

Before the Face of God: A Daily Guide for Living from the Book of Romans by R. C. Sproul. Published by Baker Book House, Grand Rapids, Michigan, 1992, with volumes based on Luke and the Old Testament also available.

Morning and Evening by Charles H. Spurgeon and edited by Roy H. Clarke. Published by Thomas Nelson Publishers, Nashville, Tennessee, 1994.

The Finishing Touch: Becoming God's Masterpiece by Charles R. Swindoll. Published by Word Publishing, Waco, Texas, 1994.

A 31-Day Experience: The Pursuit of God by A. W. Tozer, compiled by Edythe Draper. Published by Christian Publications, Camp Hill, Pennsylvania, 1995.

Renewed Day by Day by A. W. Tozer, compiled by Gerald Smith. Published in two volumes by Christian Publications, Camp Hill, Pennsylvania, 1995.

The One Year Book of Personal Prayer: Inspirational Prayers and Thoughts for Each Day of the Year. Published by Tyndale House Publishers, Wheaton, Illinois, 1991, it includes contributions from Dwight L. Moody, Peter Marshall, John Baillie, Charles Spurgeon, and many others.

BIBLES

NIV Couples' Devotional Bible. Published by Zondervan Publishing House, Grand Rapids, Michigan, 1994, it includes contributions from Gary Smalley, Charles R. Swindoll, and many others.

The Serendipity Bible Study Book, edited by Lyman Coleman, Denny Rydberg, Richard Peace, and Gary Christopherson. Published by Zondervan Publishing House, Grand Rapids, Michigan, 1988.

The Small Group Study Bible, edited by James C. Galvin. Published by Tyndale House Publishers, Wheaton, Illinois, 1995.

BIBLE STUDY HELPS:
COMMENTARIES, CONCORDANCES, DICTIONARIES

Zondervan NIV Bible Commentary, edited by Kenneth L Barker and John R. Kohnlenberger III. Published in two volumes by Zondervan Publishing House, Grand Rapids, Michigan, 1994.

New Commentary on the Whole Bible: Old Testament Volume, edited by J. D. Douglas, James K. Hoffmeier, Ted A. Hildbrandt, and Mark R. Norton. Published by Tyndale House Publishers, Wheaton, Illinois, 1990.

New Commentary on the Whole Bible: New Testament Volume, edited by J. D. Douglas and Philip W. Comfort. Published by Tyndale House Publishers, Wheaton, Illinois, 1990.

New Bible Companion, edited by Robert B. Hughes and J. Carl Laney. Published by Tyndale House Publishers, Wheaton, Illinois, 1990.

The Bible Knowledge Commentary, edited by John F. Walvoord and Roy B. Zuck. Published in two volumes by Victor Books, Wheaton, Illinois, 1983.

The New Compact Key Reference Concordance, edited by Ronald F. Youngblood. Published by Thomas Nelson Publishers, Nashville, Tennessee, 1992.

COMPACT SET

NIV Compact Dictionary of the Bible, edited by J. D. Douglas and Merrill C. Tenney. Published by Zondervan Publishing House, Grand Rapids, Michigan, 1989.

The NIV Compact Concordance, edited by John R. Kohlenberger III. Published by Zondervan Publishing House, Grand Rapids, Michigan, 1993.

NIV Compact Bible Commentary, edited by John Sailhammer. Published by Zondervan Publishing House, Grand Rapids, Michigan, 1994.

Notes

PREFACE

1. Religious News Service, "More Couples Turn to Bible for Marriage Enrichment." *Chicago Tribune*, Friday, February 10, 1995, Section: Chicagoland, p. 8.
2. Andrew Greeley, *Faithful Attraction* (New York: Tom Doherty Associates, 1991), pp. 122-138.

CHAPTER ONE:
Spiritually Two-gether

1. Andrew Greely, *Love and Play* (Chicago: The Thomas More Press, 1975), p. 64.
2. Kenneth Scott Latourette, *A History of Christianity* (New York: Harper and Brothers, 1953), p. 228.
3. Woodward, Kenneth et al, "Talking to God," *Newsweek*. (January 6, 1992), p. 42.

CHAPTER TWO:
Worshiping Two-gether

1. Lawrence J. Crabb,*The Marriage Builder* (Grand Rapids: Zondervan Publishing House, 1982), p. 32.
2. Teresa of Avila of the 16th century. Gloria Hutchinson, *Six Ways to Pray from Six Great Sainsts* (St. Anthony Messenger Press, 1982), p. 108.
3. Judson J. Swihart, *How Do You Say, "I Love You"* (Downers Grove, IL: Inter-Varsity Press, 1977), p. 43.
4. Sherod Miller, Elam E. Nunnally, Daniel B. Wackman,*Alive and Aware* (Minneapolis: Interpersonal Communications Programs, Inc., 1976), p. 149.
5. Dallas Willard, *The Spirit of the Disciplines* (San Francisco: Harper & Row, Publishers, 1988), p. 177.

6. Ibid., p.176.
7. Mike Mason, *The Mystery of Marriage* (Portland: Multnomah Press, 1985) p. 113.
8. Dorothy Day, introduction to *The Practice of the Presence of God* by Brother Lawrence of the Resurrection, translated by Donald Attwater (Springfield, IL: Templegate, 1974), p. 9,10.
9. Commentary paraphrased and quoted from Michael Green, *2 Peter and Jude, Tyndale New Testament Commentaries*, Revised Edition, Leon Morris, ed. (Leister, England: Inter-Varsity Press), pp. 205-208.

CHAPTER THREE:
Celebrating Two-gether

1. Eutychus VIII, "This Thanksgiving I'm Thankful." *Christianity Today*, (November 17, 1978) p. 8.
2. Paul Stevens, p. 15.
3. Jean Calvin. *Calvin's Commentaries: The Epistle of Paul the Apostle to the Hebrew and the First and Second Epistles of St. Peter*. Translated by William B. Johnston (Grand Rapids: Eerdmans, 1963), p. 234.
4. John R. Yungblut, *Rediscovering Prayer* (New York: The Seabury Press, 1972), p. 85.
5. A college board recently invited the million high school seniors who took its aptitude test to indicate "how you feel you compare with other people your own age in certain areas of ability." It appears that American high school seniors are not whacked with inferiority feelings. While 60 percent reported themselves as better than average in athletic ability, only 6 percent felt themselves to be below average. In leadership ability, 70 percent rated themselves as above average, 2 percent below average. In ability to get along with others, 0 percent of the 829,000 students who responded rated themselves below average, 60 percent rated themselves in the top 10 percent , and 25 percent saw themselves among the top 1 percent. (Meyers, David C. "A New Look at Pride," *Your Better Self*. San Francisco: Harper & Row, Publishers, 1983), p. 84.

CHAPTER FOUR:
Praying Two-gether

1. Woodward, Kenneth et al, "Talking to God," *Newsweek*. (January 6, 1992), p. 40.
2. Paul Hinnebusch, *Prayer, the Search for Authenticity* (New York: Sheed and Ward, 1969), p. 22.
3. Richard J. Foster, *Celebration of Discipline* (New York: Harper & Row, 1978), p. 30.
4. Willard, *The Spirit of the Disciplines*, p. 184.

5. Gil Peterson, ed., "Manipulation or Ministry," *Family Life Education* (Wheaton, Il: Scripture Press Ministries, 1978, p. 14.
6. Hinnebusch, *Prayer, The Search for Authenticity*, p. vi.
7. Elijah, though God promised him it would rain, nonetheless continued to pray for it (1 Kings 18:42). He is only one of many examples in Scripture where promises were claimed by prayer.
8. Judson Cornwall, *Meeting God* (Altamonte Springs: Creation House, 1988), p. 80.
9. Rahner, Karl, and Johann B. Metz, *The Courage to Pray* (New York: Crossroad, 1981), p. 12.
10. Ibid., p. 13.
11. Foster, *Celebration of Discipline*, p. 19
12. Ibid, p. 27,28.
13. Woodward, Kenneth et al, "Talking to God," p. 44.
14. Foster, *Celebration of Discipline*, p. 15.

CHAPTER FIVE:
Studying Two-gether

1. Foster, *Celebration of Discipline*, p. 55.
2. Michael E. Ruane. "Jury Renders Guilty Verdict Against 'God's Law,'" *Chicago Tribune*. Monday, August 20, 1984. section 5, pp. 1, 8.